FOCUS

A MEMOIR

BY

INGRID RICKS

Kristen,

Thank you for making
This such a great year
for Hannah. Here's to
embracing the moment
& focusing on what counts.
♡ Ingrid

1

LATE JANUARY - 2004

THERE WAS SOMETHING wrong with the machine.

For the past five minutes, I'd been staring into a large, box-shaped medical device, waiting to have my peripheral vision checked. The eye doctor's assistant, a thin, blonde woman with a chin-length bob and caked-on makeup, told me that all I had to do was press on the clicker I was holding whenever I saw a white dot flash anywhere inside that metal box. Simple enough. Except that after pressing my forehead against the headrest for so long I felt a crease forming, I still hadn't seen a flashing dot.

"When are you going to start the test?" I finally asked the woman, still pushing my forehead against the headrest. I needed to get it over with so I could pick up my five-year-old daughter from her Montessori school and get her to a children's music group audition twenty miles away.

"It's been going for a while," she replied. She was young—no more than twenty-three or twenty-four. I couldn't see her face now because of the box I was staring into, but I imagined it was blank and a bit dazed. She was probably thinking about where she was going to party that evening, and the idea that she was so checked out she couldn't even properly administer the test irked me. I jerked my head away from the box and shot her an annoyed look.

"Well, it's not working then, because nothing is happening."

I stepped out of the way so the assistant could check it out for herself. She positioned herself on the stool, pushed her forehead against the headrest, and gazed through the small window into the box.

"It seems to be working fine for me," she announced a minute later, pushing herself away from the machine and resuming her testing position. "Why don't we try it again?"

Her words jarred me. And something about the way she said them felt like a thousand tiny needles all jamming into my skin at once. She didn't look at me when she talked, but I could tell it wasn't out of complacency. She suddenly seemed very attentive and serious—and I liked this version of her even less. For the first time since I had heard the words *degenerative eye disease* the day before, panic shot through me. I took my seat in front of the metal box and picked up the clicker.

"Ready?" she asked.

"Yeah."

I waited for the flashing lights. Nothing. My stomach was a tangle of knots and they were pulling so tight I could hardly breathe. I jerked my forehead back from the headrest a second time and stood up from the stool.

"It's just not working," I declared, trying to keep my voice steady.

"I'm going to get the doctor," the assistant mumbled. "Why don't you just take a seat in the chair?"

My body found its way into the black reclining patient chair. I could feel my hands shaking but I couldn't stop them. I didn't want the eye doctor to see me cry but I couldn't keep the tears in. The meaning of his quiet, serious words from the previous day were suddenly taking hold.

The eye doctor walked into the room and put his hand on my knee. He didn't speak for a few minutes; he just left his hand there while I sobbed. He was about my age—somewhere in his mid-to-late thirties—and only twenty-four hours earlier, we were joking and swapping stories about our toddlers. Now, he was patting my leg and comforting me like I was a toddler myself.

"We already knew this wasn't going to be good," he started out slowly, carefully choosing his words.

What do you mean, WE? I wanted to shout back. It's true he had told me that the spidery pigment he saw when he looked into the back of my eyes resembled something he referred to as Retinitis Pigmentosa. And when I Googled the foreign-sounding words later that evening, some of the symptoms—such as night blindness and loss of peripheral vision—matched what I had been experiencing. But the information I found online also said it was a hereditary disease and, as far as I knew, not a single person in my extended family had anything like this. What's more, the information I found said that people with RP were legally blind by age forty, but at thirty-seven, I had perfect 20/20 vision. Then there was the final bit of information that had made me turn off my computer—the part about losing all remaining eyesight by your mid-fifties. I reminded myself that the eye doctor had told me he was only guessing at the RP diagnosis. Clearly he had made a mistake.

"We don't have to do this today if you don't want to," the eye doctor continued in a gentle tone. "Either way, the end result is the same. I need to send you to a retinal specialist."

He pulled a stool next to me, sat down, and handed me tissues to catch the flood of water escaping my eyes. It was humiliating to have him see me like this, and in a desperate attempt to end my blubbering, I bit my lip so hard that it started bleeding. In my mind, I debated whether the test was even necessary. The doctor already knew the answer and at this point, I knew it too.

"Let's do it," I said after finally calming down enough to speak. "I want to know where I'm at."

"Are you sure?" he asked. I could hear the hesitation in his voice and sensed he was already bracing himself for my next meltdown.

"Yeah. I'm sure."

The eye doctor left the room and the assistant appeared a minute later to administer the test. She avoided looking at me. It was clear she wanted this over as much as I did.

I pressed my now-swollen eyes up to the peephole for a third time and once again held the clicker in my hand. After about ten minutes the test was done and the assistant left. A few minutes later, the eye doctor was back with my test results—displayed in the form of two 8 ½ x 11 sheets of paper.

"These two pieces of paper represent your field of vision—which in a healthy person is ninety degrees in each eye," he explained in the same gentle, quiet voice I now knew to associate with bad news. "The area in black ink is the area where you've lost your vision. The unmarked area represents the vision you have left."

I stared at the two pieces of paper he had placed in front of me. They were both covered in black ink, with an untouched circle in the center of each and a sliver of white that looked like a big smiley-face underneath each eye. The top of one sheet contained the words Left Eye. The other sheet was titled Right Eye.

"So what does this mean?" I asked, not sure I wanted to hear the answer. "How much do I have left?"

"About ten degrees in each eye," he returned, not looking at me.

I had heard all I needed to hear. During my Internet research the night before, I had read that a person with a ten-degree visual field or less in each eye is considered legally blind.

"I have to go now," I managed. I jumped out of the chair and sprinted to the door. There was no way I was going to let him see me lose it again.

I held back the wailing sobs until I reached my car, locked myself in, and laid my head against the steering wheel. I had experienced fear plenty of times in my life. But it was nothing compared to the terror that was now gripping me.

I don't know how much time elapsed. But it suddenly hit me that I needed to pick up my five-year-old daughter, Syd, at her Montessori school. I was supposed to take a twenty-minute drive on a busy interstate to get her to the children's music group auditions she had been asking me about all week. After that, I needed to battle the freeway traffic back to North Bend, the rural town where we lived, so I could pick up my other daughter, Hannah, who was about to turn two, from her daycare. Then I needed to stop by the grocery store, pick up some food, head home and make dinner.

I had to pull myself together. I had to think. But I was in such a fog I was having a hard time remembering how to breathe.

What was I supposed to do?

All I wanted to do was curl up in a ball in the back seat of my car and go to sleep so I could wake up and discover that this was all just a bad dream.

I kept my head resting against the steering wheel for a few more minutes, unable to will myself to move. Then it occurred to me to call John.

I grabbed my phone and punched in the numbers to my husband's cell phone. I got his voicemail.

"John. I'm going blind," I sobbed into the handset. "I'm practically already blind."

2

Had I been even vaguely aware that degenerative eye diseases could afflict a person before the age of eighty, I would have noticed the signs a long time before my first-ever eye exam uncovered that I was already legally blind.

For years I'd had problems seeing in the dark and I was always bumping into things. Once, nearly six years before my diagnosis, I'd plowed through a waist-high vegetable stand in a grocery store because I didn't see it. Vegetables went flying and my friend, Doug, started laughing so hard I was sure the people glaring at us thought I had done it on purpose.

"You are without a doubt the most tunnel-focused person I have ever met," he stated when he finally caught his breath.

I smiled when he said this because I knew it was true. I had a reputation for locking in on goals and going after them—oblivious to anything else in my path. And I was proud of it. It's what had enabled me to escape my rocky home life and put myself through college. It's what had launched my successful freelance writing career and gotten me to Africa to write for a relief organization.

It's what had landed me a great position at the advertising agency where I worked at the time with Doug.

Because I was always consumed with the goal in front of me, I was absent-minded about everything else. So it made sense to me that I would occasionally bump into people because I didn't notice they were there or that I would sometimes leave a sweater or bag behind at a friend's house. And while my night-blindness was annoying, I didn't think anything of that because I knew plenty of people had a difficult time seeing at night. But over the past year, I had noticed a weird depth perception issue that kept creeping up on me. Six months before my diagnosis, I had gone hiking with a couple of girlfriends and couldn't keep up. I kept tripping over rocks and tree roots on the trail and felt so clumsy that I started watching my feet every step I took to ensure I didn't fall.

"Go ahead, I'll catch up," I'd urged them, even though I felt betrayed when they left me behind. It was even worse on the way down. I had to inch my way off that mountain, and my friends both completed the three-mile hike a full half-hour ahead of me.

At Christmas time, just a few weeks before I'd finally visited an eye doctor, I had gone to a friend's holiday party and had such a difficult time parallel parking that the woman waiting to park behind me was convinced I had snuck in a few pre-party drinks.

I spent a full ten minutes trying to park my Volkswagen Passat alongside the residential curb. But no matter how hard I tried, I just couldn't get my car close enough to keep it out of the street.

For a while the woman just sat in her SUV, shooting me dirty looks. After watching me hop out of my car for the third time to check out the distance between my car and the curb, she'd finally had enough.

"Look. Do you want me to guide you?" she yelled out into the cold December air.

I felt hot embarrassment wash over me.

"Yeah, that would be great," I returned, trying to laugh it off. "Don't know what's up with me today."

Even then it didn't occur to me that something was seriously wrong. It didn't even hit me that I had a problem a week after the holiday party incident, when I sideswiped a car on the freeway after I'd looked into the dark, rainy night and saw nothing. It wasn't until I played racquetball with my husband to celebrate my thirty-seventh birthday in mid-January that I realized I could probably use glasses. No matter how hard I tried, I couldn't score a point on him. Not that I had ever actually beat him at the game. But I used to be able to hold my own.

"You are doing it all wrong," John coached, trying to keep his voice patient since it was, after all, my birthday. "You can't track the ball with your eyes. You've got to pick a spot on the wall and catch it with your peripheral vision."

"Okay, if you say so," I replied.

I followed John's advice and stared at a spot in the center of the wall. When balls started whizzing by my head, he sounded alarmed.

"Did you seriously not see that?" he asked. "It was only about six inches away from your head. You've really got to get your eyes checked."

I laughed at his frustration but agreed to make an eye appointment. Both of my parents wore glasses and I figured age was catching up to me. A week later, I was waiting in the lobby at the local ophthalmologist's office. I arrived early so I had plenty of time to browse through the frames. I figured that if I was going to be wearing glasses, I wanted to look good. By the time I was summoned into the exam room by the thin blonde assistant, I had already picked out a cute pair of red cat-eye frames and had asked the receptionist at the front desk to hold them for me. It never crossed my mind that I had an eye problem that no glasses—regardless of how good they looked on me—were going to fix.

My daughter never made it to the children's music group tryouts. After finally reaching John, I drove myself home from the eye doctor's office and spent most of the next week huddled in the darkness of our downstairs family room.

I was so shocked and scared I was paralyzed.

For the first time in my life, I noticed what I didn't see. Now, every time I looked at Syd and Hannah, I realized that I could see their faces but I couldn't see the rest of their bodies or anything else around them. If I wanted to walk down a flight of stairs, I noticed that I had to keep my eyes glued on my feet and the steps below or I couldn't see where I was going. When it was dark, I couldn't see anything—not even my hand when I held it up in front of my face.

I saw the same things that I saw the day before. But everything had changed. I was legally blind. And it was only a matter of time before it all went dark.

In my mind, I saw a blind woman with a white cane slowly feeling her way down the street. She looked unkempt; her hair was going every which way and her clothes were outdated and didn't match. People were staring at her with pity and some even wore a look of disgust. Others crossed the street to avoid her. The woman kept inching her way down the block, pushing the white cane in front of her to find the cracks and curbs, listening to the traffic zooming past her and trying to figure out where to step next.

When that thought became too painful to follow, my mind drifted back to junior high and the "What's Worse" game I once played with a friend at a sleepover.

"Okay, choose," my friend had said. "Deaf or blind?"

She acted like it was a tough decision.

"Are you kidding me? Deaf," I nearly shouted at her. "If you're deaf you can still read lips. You can still get around. Sure—it's a little inconvenient. But it's not like it's the end of the world. If you're blind, you're screwed."

Blind people terrified me. Every tap of their white cane or movement of their seeing-eye dog reminded me that they'd been robbed. Not just of being able to see the sun rising over the mountains or watching squirrels climb trees or taking in the wonder of the ocean. Or even to make sure that they were having a good hair day. They had been robbed of their freedom and independence—the two essentials that I felt defined a person. The idea that I was quickly becoming one of them, already was one of them to some degree, was enough to send me over the edge.

I snapped back into the present, curled up in the corner of that dark family room. Syd and Hannah were upstairs with John but I was having a hard time facing them. The idea that I would soon not be able to see them at all was so painful it hurt to look at them.

How was I going to take care of them? What if I couldn't see them grow up? Watch them dance? Admire their artwork? See them grow into teenagers and adults? What if I couldn't see their prom dates or take in the expressions on their faces when they were happy or sad or angry? How would they deal with having a blind mom? Would they be ashamed of me?

The more my mind locked in on my future blindness, the more the terror gripped me.

What was the point of living in a world that I couldn't see? John and I had just finished remodeling our house. We had gutted the kitchen and living room and had installed maple floors, Shaker cabinets, and French doors. It was beautiful but what did it matter if I couldn't see it? What about every other beautiful thing I would miss out on? What about not being able to see myself?

I curled into a ball, rocking myself as I let my mind go to the next unbearable thought: how was I going to work?

In four weeks, I would be heading to Africa to write about children orphaned by AIDS. I had been hired by a nonprofit organization to put together a collection of stories for a publication that would go out to potential donors. It was a rare dream of an opportunity amid the steady, somewhat dry marketing communications work that now took up most of my time.

How could I write the stories I cared about if I couldn't see the people I was writing about? How could I get on a plane to meet with clients if I couldn't see where I was going?

In my now ongoing personal terror sessions, I always saved my worst fears for last: my independence and my relationship with John.

John and I hadn't had a single discussion about my eyesight since my diagnosis a few days earlier. We just didn't talk about it. I was too upset to bring it up and maybe he was too. Most of his time was spent logging hours at the law firm where he worked. The girls were both in preschool during the day—giving me eight hours to huddle in our dark basement thinking about my fate. In the evenings, when I managed to pull myself upstairs to make dinner and go through the motions of being a mom, we just made small talk.

Yeah, John definitely wasn't talking about it. But then, what was there to really say? His wife was going blind. He was going to be stuck with a blind person. He was going to have to take care of me and look after me—like a little kid. What kind of quality of life was that? For either of us?

The idea that I could become a burden to John was the final straw. I just couldn't go there. I wouldn't let it happen. That left a scenario that was too difficult for my brain to process: John gone from my life, and me—housebound, blind and alone.

3

A WEEK AFTER MY initial eye appointment, John took the afternoon off from work and drove me to Seattle—a forty-minute car ride from North Bend—to see the retinal specialist my eye doctor had recommended. He was one of only a few eye specialists in the Pacific Northwest who dealt with Retinitis Pigmentosa, which I now knew was a rare eye disease that afflicted only one in every 4,000 people.

Soon after checking in at the reception desk, I was summoned to a small room for yet another visual field test while John waited outside. Now that I knew what I was in for, I just gritted my teeth, grabbed the clicker and pounded through it. Once done, John and I were escorted to a waiting area full of people with serious-looking eye problems. One guy had a patch over his right eye and puss oozing out of his left one. Another-ancient looking man wore sunglasses and had a white cane. I did a quick scan of the rest of the people. They all appeared to be over the age of seventy.

"Looks like it's going to be a while," I whispered to John as we settled into our seats.

I saw a woman in a white lab coat walk by with some paperwork in her hand. She knocked on a door across the hall from the waiting area. I watched her open the door and stick in her head. I could hear a few muffled words but couldn't make out what they were. A minute later, the woman pulled her head out of the doorway, shut it, and turned to look at all of us. I felt her eyes settle on me.

"Ingrid Ricks?"

My heart sank. Why was she calling my name? Everyone else had been waiting a lot longer than I had. This didn't make sense.

By this point I had done enough research to know that I likely had one of two things: RP or a brain tumor. Neither of them sounded particularly appealing to me but if I had to choose, I decided RP was probably the better of the two options. But now I was nervous. Really nervous. Because based on the serious look on the woman's face and the fact that I had catapulted to the front of the line, I knew that the information contained in the paperwork she was holding wasn't good.

John and I followed the woman into an exam room. A minute later, the technician who had run the visual field test popped in. He was Asian, around thirty, and had a friendly smile.

"So what did you find? What did the tests say?" I asked anxiously.

"Well, I can't really discuss it with you—that's for the doctor."

"Do I have a brain tumor?"

I didn't mean to sound so blunt, but if I was dying from brain cancer I wanted this guy to suck it up and tell me.

The guy looked at me like I was a little nuts.

"No. At least not that I'm aware of," he finally answered. "But before we can really confirm your eye problems, we are going to do an ERG to get a better snapshot of your retina."

As he squeezed a few eye drops into my eyes to dilate them, he explained that an ERG—short for electroretinography—was a test that measured the retina's electrical response. The retina, he explained, was found in the back of the eye and was responsible for converting and sending images to the brain. I'd never thought about the parts that made up my eye. I just took it for granted that when I opened my eyelids each morning, I could see.

Once my eyes were sufficiently dilated and then numbed with anesthetic drops, the technician escorted me to the ERG testing facility. I entered the first of two rooms and took a seat in a black patient chair as directed by the female lab technician who greeted me.

"What I'm going to do is attach this electrode to your right eye so we can measure the electrical response in your retina," she explained, holding up a tiny device that resembled a contact lens. "We'll only test one eye because that's enough for us to get a sense for what's going on."

I spent the next few minutes trying to pretend that it was completely normal for the woman to pry open my right eyelid with a speculum and then stick the electrode onto my eyeball. Once that electrode was secured, she attached another tiny electrode on the skin just underneath my eye—which I later learned was necessary to provide a ground for the very faint electrical signals produced by the retina.

I took a deep breath, trying to keep myself calm by imagining I was lying on a beach somewhere getting a facial massage. I didn't really have a clamp stretching my eyelid open or an electrode attached to my eyeball. And that glaring light overhead was really just the sun.

"We'll have you go into the next room, which we seal so it's completely dark," the technician explained while making last-minute adjustments to the electrodes. "You will wait there for about twenty minutes while your eyes adjust to the dark. Then we'll flash lights and the recording device will enable us to measure what is being captured by your retina."

Forget the sandy beach. I was in a torture chamber. Even the light in this room was hurting my dilated eyes, and the gadget that was keeping my right eye propped open made it impossible to blink.

I followed the woman into the room and took a seat on another black chair. Then she flipped off the lights and shut the door. Everything went black. It was a thick black nothingness. Even darker than the darkness I was used to at night. So this was what it was like to be blind. Thick black nothing.

I was jolted out of my sinking sadness by the strobe lights that I was certain were really semi-truck headlights that began flashing into my eyeballs. Maybe the anesthetic drops were already wearing off, because the excruciating burn of the glare felt like acid being thrown into my eye. My eyelid strained against the clamp holding it in place.

I would have cried but my right eye was stretched open so wide it was about ready to pop out of my head. And for some reason, my left eye seemed incapable of making tears without the blinking capability of my right eye.

I don't know how long the torture session lasted because every second seemed like an hour. But finally the semi-truck headlights were turned off, the clamp was taken out of my eye, and the electrodes were removed. Then I was escorted back to the patient room where John was waiting for me.

"That was hell," I whispered. "I'm surprised they didn't give me electrical shocks while I was in there."

When the eye doctor entered the room a few minutes later, he was holding my test results in his hand.

He was older—probably mid-sixties, with silver hair and a slim build. He didn't smile when he introduced himself, which was bad enough. But then he had the nerve to shake John's hand but not mine.

"Well, your ERG is consistent with Retinitis Pigmentosa, and confirms what we found in your visual field test," he started out, his eyes finally resting on mine. "Why haven't you been in to get your eyes checked before?"

His words stung. I was here for some help, not a reprimand.

"Because I could always see fine," I snapped.

"My eyesight has always been 20/20 on the driver's license test," I added, suddenly feeling compelled to prove that I wasn't an idiot. "How was I supposed to know something was wrong? I thought I had perfect vision."

John quickly jumped in.

"So can you tell us more about what Retinitis Pigmentosa is and what causes it?" he asked.

The doctor seemed relieved to be able to turn his attention back to John.

"With RP, something causes the photoreceptor cells to die, leaving a spidery pigment that blocks light from getting to the retina," he explained. "It's a hereditary disease but what makes it so difficult to track is that there are numerous genes tied to RP."

The retinal specialist looked back at me.

"Do you mind if I have a couple of residents take a look at your eyes?" he asked. "This is a teaching hospital and real-life examples are much more educational than a textbook."

I shrugged. Minutes later, a string of residents crowded around the doctor, anxious for a peek into my diseased eyes.

The retinal specialist reclined my chair so far back that I was nearly staring at the ceiling. He told me to open my eyes as wide as I could. Then he shined the same semi-truck headlight into my eyes. Only this time there wasn't a clamp to keep them open.

"See all that spidery pigment back there?" I heard him explain to the doctors-in-training, who were all gawking into my eyes. I tried to keep my eyelids from involuntarily closing to protect my eyes from the excruciating glare. I felt the doctor's fingers on my eyelids, prying them open into the headlight looming above me. I felt the residents huddling in around me—their hot, smelly breath on my face.

"This is a classic case of RP," the retinal specialist continued. "As it gets into the advanced stages, as you can see here, the pigment takes over the eye until it blocks all usable incoming light from getting to the retina."

My heart jumped. What did he mean 'advanced stages'?

I waited until his impromptu seminar was over and everyone was gone before asking him the question.

"Well, you are in a pretty advanced stage at this point," he said. "I would put you at about ten degrees in each eye, which makes you legally blind."

I took a deep breath. I already knew that part. What I needed to know was how I could keep it from advancing further. Over the past week, during the times I had managed to snap out of my depression enough to do something productive, I had spent my time glued to the computer, researching every possible bit of information I could find on Retinitis Pigmentosa and possible treatments. I had come across studies that had indicated that large doses of Vitamin A coupled with Omega 3 seemed to help slow the progression. I had also read that Lutein was essential for eyes.

Given that this guy was the expert, I felt that he could steer me in the right direction.

"Yeah, I know about the legally blind part," I replied, trying not to sound impatient. "But I can live with that if I can stop the progression. I've read that nutritional supplements are really beginning to help. Which supplements do you recommend?"

For about thirty seconds, he didn't say anything. Instead, he grabbed a pen and scribbled something down on a piece of paper.

"I've not come across a single vitamin or anything else that's made a bit of difference with this," he said flatly, not looking at me as he shoved the scrap of paper into my hand. "The nearest viable treatment is at least twenty years out and it's not likely to help you because it will be too late by then. I'm sorry."

I looked at the piece of paper and almost threw up. He had written down the words Center for the Blind with a phone number scrawled next to it.

It took every ounce of self-control I had not to wad it up and throw it at him.

I sucked in my breath, trying to get air.

"What about driving?" I blurted.

Driving was more than just a necessity for me. It was a way of life. I had spent my teenage years living on the highways of the Midwest with my dad, hustling tools out of the back of whatever beat-up pickup he was driving at the time. In my twenties, to support my freelance writing career, I had once again teamed up with my dad—this time hustling telecom services to truckers. But since by then I was old enough to drive, I hit the highways and freeways of the Midwest on my own. I had crisscrossed the country several times in my economy model Plymouth Sundance, hanging up marketing flyers in truck stops and sleeping in the back of my car in truck stops or rest areas each evening. An open highway represented freedom to me and the idea that I couldn't just get in my car, hit the gas pedal and go was like ripping my heart out.

The doctor had already started moving toward the door. He turned his head back over his shoulder to look at me.

"You seem like an intelligent person," he said. "What do you think?"

John and I didn't talk on the drive home. I felt like I had been run over by the semi-truck that must have been attached to the headlights the doctor had beamed into my eyes. I didn't know what John was thinking. And I wasn't sure I wanted to know.

I spent the rest of the afternoon numbing my pain with wine. My mind was so jumbled with terrifying thoughts that I couldn't concentrate on any of them. I knew I needed to get a handle on this. But how was I supposed to handle being blind?

That night, I received a call from my dad.

"So help me understand what you can see," he said. "When I look at the center of a wall, I see both ends of the wall. Is that what you see?"

"No, Dad," I returned sharply, not even trying to hide the anger in my voice. "When I look at the center of the wall, I see the center of the wall. That's it."

Silence screamed through the phone.

I knew he was just trying to reach out to me. And I knew I wasn't being kind. But the last thing I needed was a reminder that my dad, who never had a problem seeing in the first place, now had perfect vision thanks to his recent Lasik surgery. Vision problems were supposed to happen to people who were old. Not to people in their thirties. And right now I was too angry to care about how I came across to others.

"Look," he said finally. "It's hard to know what to say and what not to say. I feel like I'm walking on eggshells here. I really do."

There was more silence. I recognized that I was supposed to jump in and rescue the conversation—apologize for being so impossible. But I just couldn't.

My dad once again broke the silence.

"Look. I know what you are going through is hard. And I admit that it would be really tough to lose my eyesight. But let me tell you something I know for an absolute certainty. I can tell you that when something is taken away from you like this, something else is given to you in its place."

It took everything I had inside me to keep from exploding. Four years earlier, my dad had lost his business. It was a business he had spent a decade building and at the time, it had meant everything to him. But he hadn't lost his health. He wasn't going blind. He could still build another business. It wasn't the same thing.

"I've got to go, Dad," I said quietly. "I've got to figure out my life."

4

THOUGH NEITHER OF us seemed capable of talking about our emotions, or what my fading eyesight meant to our relationship and life, the one thing John and I could focus on was the immediate next step—moving.

He brought it up.

"I guess we need to start looking for a house in Seattle," he announced as soon as I had ended the call with my dad. "I'll ask my parents if we can borrow the money for a down payment."

If I hadn't been so angry over my circumstances, I would have laughed at the irony of this.

For the past few years, John and I had been living in a rural community thirty-five miles east of Seattle. We had wanted to buy a house in Seattle in the first place but with John fresh out of law school and only working part-time as a legal assistant while studying for the bar, it had been out of our price range. Our plan when we bought our house was to live in it for five years while we got on our feet financially, and then move back to the city. But we never could seem to get ahead enough to make that happen.

Just a month before my diagnosis, we had officially reached that five-year mark and John and I talked about what it would take to move back to Seattle.

"You know I want it as much as you do," John had said at the time. "But we just can't afford it. Maybe when the girls are grown and out on their own, we can sell the house and buy a condo downtown."

I had accepted his argument despite the nagging ache in my gut because I knew he was right. We were broke and had no way to swing a move.

But now, because of my newly discovered eye disease, staying put wasn't a choice. We didn't just live in a rural community. We lived in the mountains five miles away from the nearest grocery store or gas station. I had to get on a busy road just to get our daughters to their respective preschools. And it was only going to get more challenging once Syd started kindergarten in the fall. We needed to be in Seattle, in a neighborhood where schools were within walking distance and bus service was within easy access.

If I could find a silver lining in this stupid eye disease, this was it.

After crunching numbers, we quickly figured out that we were better off turning our existing house into a rental for a while until we could get established in a new house and then sell when the market was right. But that meant we needed a short-term loan to cover a down payment.

"Okay, wish me luck," John said as he sat down next to me and dialed his parents' number.

I listened as John asked his dad if he would be willing to loan us the money. John had already filled his parents in on my eye diagnosis so they understood the circumstances we faced. I could hear his dad through the receiver, telling John that it would be no problem—he was glad to be able to help us out. I breathed a sigh of relief. But then I heard the pause and his next words.

"I know you're good for it," his dad said. "The only thing I'm concerned about is if something happens to you."

Another pause.

"I mean, I really hope nothing would ever happen to you. But if something did, I'm not sure how Ingrid could repay it given her situation."

His words knocked the air out of me. What did he mean *I'm not sure how Ingrid could repay it?* The one thing that I had always been was responsible. I had always paid my way—always. I was the one who had mostly been keeping John and me afloat since we'd been married—supporting him through law school, bar exams, and the slow uphill grind of establishing his law practice. I'd pay a person back if I had to sell everything I owned and dig ditches for the rest of my life. Then again, it sounded like that's what his dad worried about—my inability to even dig ditches. Is this how people thought of me now? Already? I was already a liability?

"Oh, don't worry about that," I heard John say into the phone. "We have life insurance and I can make sure that you are first on the list. And once the market improves and we're ready to sell our current house, you'll be the first to be repaid."

I felt my hands curl into fists. I was clenching them so hard I could feel my fingernails digging into my palms and could see them turning white.

"What was that about?" I asked as soon as John hung up the phone.

"Oh, nothing," he replied.

"That's bullshit," I snapped. "Why didn't you stand up for me? Why didn't you tell him that I could and would take care of any obligations? I mean I always have. You know that."

John looked ready to explode.

"What did you expect me to do?" he shot back, exasperated. "We need them to loan us the money. My dad doesn't mean anything by it. He's just voicing their concern. They have a right to know how they are going to get paid back and I told them. It's not a big deal."

I could feel the heat burning in my cheeks. I tried to steady myself by staring straight ahead and taking a deep breath.

John's dad was a kind, generous man who was also very logical—a trait that John had inherited. He was retired on a fixed income and while he wanted to help us, he needed to make sure he would be repaid. I knew on an intellectual level that John was right. His dad was just asking the questions that he felt needed to be asked. I also knew his words weren't intended for me to hear. But they ripped at me like a knife. Being viewed as a worthless, helpless human being was what I feared more than anything. And it was already happening.

"Look," John said, his voice more patient. "I know you're good for it. Who cares what anyone else thinks? We just have to get through this."

John took the next day off from work and we headed to Seattle to house-hunt. Our budget was tight, but we didn't realize how tight until we began touring the houses in our price range. The first place we checked out had been a student rental and looked like it had been used as a frat party house. The walls were so dirty they were more gray than white and were punctured with holes. The floors were covered with a filthy, matted, green carpet that reeked of beer and marijuana, and the rooms were so tiny and boxy they looked like they had each been divided in half to create space for more tenants.

The next place we looked at was a tall, skinny townhouse on a busy arterial with no yard, making it impossible with two small children.

"We might be in trouble," John muttered as we climbed into our car and followed the realtor to the next house on our list.

I didn't reply. We had to be in Seattle and I couldn't allow myself to get discouraged.

The next few houses we looked at repeated the pattern— decent on the inside but in a horrible, unlivable neighborhood. Or in a good neighborhood but unlivable on the inside.

We wrapped up our day with the realtor and considered heading home. But on a whim, we decided to drive to Ballard—a neighborhood we loved in northwest Seattle—to check out a mid-1960s home we had found on the Internet.

The pictures on the Internet weren't bad and the house met our three-bedroom, two-bathroom requirement. We called the realtor associated with the house and she agreed to meet us there.

"There must be something seriously wrong with it if it's still available, but it's worth a shot," I said to John as we made our way across town toward the house.

Just driving through the Ballard neighborhood excited me. Once a Scandinavian fishing village, Ballard had a beach that I loved, and because it had been a stand-alone town before being annexed to the city of Seattle, it had its own retail sector with a variety of shops and restaurants. The main street even had a movie theater. The idea that I could walk to everything I needed was exhilarating.

Within the mile that separated the retail area from the house, I counted three coffee shops. Only four blocks to go, we passed an elementary school with a large play area. Next to the school sat the neighborhood community center.

I wanted to pinch myself.

"This area is so perfect for us," I said to John, trying not to hyperventilate from my excitement.

"I agree, but don't get your hopes up," he replied.

The house sat in the center of a tree-lined block next to a turn-of-the century home brimming with the character and style John and I loved.

Our prospective house was built in 1965. The front exterior was made up of fake brick and cream-colored siding. It didn't look big from the outside. But when we stepped inside, we discovered a roomy open layout separated by a divider wall. On the left side of the divider was a large living room/dining room area with a fireplace. On the right side of the divider was a long hallway that led to three bedrooms and a bathroom with a pink toilet and matching pink bathtub. We discovered another half bathroom, this one featuring a blue toilet and matching sink, tucked into a corner of the largest bedroom.

I felt a rush of excitement. This place was clean, had plenty of room, and was in an amazing neighborhood.

The kitchen, which sat behind the living room, came with holes in the yellow linoleum and the original 1965 wall oven. A slider door opened to a rickety wood deck with a green fiberglass roof. The deck would definitely have to go. It didn't even have bars in the railing to keep the kids from falling off. What's more, the plywood that held the deck together was so dry and splintering I wasn't sure if it would even hold us all.

I tried to shut this out of my mind as the realtor led us back inside and took us downstairs to a half-finished basement. The same new cream-colored carpet that covered the upstairs flooring led to a family room with another fireplace. Unlike the freshly painted white walls above, the basement walls were covered in dark wood paneling. The basement also contained a dilapidated closet of a bathroom just big enough for a toilet, sink, and a freestanding shower stall with mold growing inside. Next to the bathroom was another small bedroom.

From a cosmetic side of things, the house needed work. But everything else about it was perfect.

I grabbed John's hand and squeezed it to get his attention. "This is it," I whispered.

"I know," he whispered back. "But don't act too excited. It would be nice to talk them down in price."

The house shouldn't have been available. It was priced at an amount we could afford in a neighborhood that should have been well out of our price range. It was as though someone had been saving it for us.

John and I made an offer on the house that evening. A couple of days later, we had a deal. We scheduled the closing date for five weeks out—the day after I was to return from Africa.

I was thrilled about the prospect of starting a new life in Seattle, and for the next two weeks, my excitement kept me from thinking about the reason behind the move. But as soon as I boarded the plane for South Africa, I felt the heavy depression take over me again.

Every time I looked out the window—first taking in the mountain peaks we flew over and then staring into the clouds as we passed over the Atlantic Ocean—it hit me that this was probably the last time I was going to be able to take a trip like this.

No one was saying it, but it was clear to me that the whole purpose of going to Africa and visiting with children orphaned by AIDS was to *see* the situation for myself. I needed to capture the images in words that would resonate with donors so they would contribute the necessary money to help these children. How was I going to write about these orphaned children and share their stories if I couldn't see them?

I landed in Johannesburg and spent the evening people-watching from the patio of a small hotel. I loved observing strangers—particularly in foreign countries—and for a while, I managed to immerse myself in the moment before remembering that soon I wouldn't be able to people-watch either. I downed my glass of wine, headed for my room, and crawled into bed.

The next morning, I boarded a small prop plane for a short flight to Nelspruit, a northeastern city known internationally for its proximity to Kruger National Park, one of the largest wild game reserves in Africa. Suzanne, the International Director for the African Children's Choir, met me at the airport.

I loved Suzanne. She was one of the kindest people I knew. She was also funny. The two of us had traveled to Sudan together a decade before and had forged a friendship over the years. She was the one overseeing the magazine for the donors and had coordinated the assignment for me.

Suzanne stood about five-feet-nine—towering over my petite five-foot-two frame. She was also about fifteen years older than I was but I never felt the age difference when we were together.

"I've got a surprise for you," she beamed as we climbed into the car. "Guess what I've discovered here—Seattle Coffee Company!"

Suzanne understood my eye disease. Though she wasn't losing her vision, her eyesight was so bad that she was nearly blind without her glasses. And like me, she struggled with night blindness. It was nice to be with someone who had at least some understanding of what I was going through.

We drove to a small, upscale shopping center and plopped down the equivalent of ten dollars for our drinks. Then, with our twelve-ounce mochas in hand, the two of us embarked on an hour-and-a-half drive to a village near the border of Swaziland, a world where a shopping mall or store of any kind was as unthinkable as a spaceship full of Martians.

The region was known for its AIDS pandemic. At the time, it was estimated that at least forty percent of the population was HIV-positive.

"It's destitute there," Suzanne cautioned as we drove. "I've never experienced anything like it. The people are so poor and so many of them are sick and dying. And as a result, there are thousands of orphaned children who have been left to fend for themselves."

I had done some research before coming and knew the problem was overwhelming. The devastating pain of losing the parents they loved and depended on was just the beginning of the nightmare for these children. So many adults were dying from AIDS that many of the orphans didn't have relatives to take them in. As a result, many of the children were forced to figure out how to survive on their own. Just scavenging enough food to get by each day was a full-time job. Then there was the task of finding shelter and staying safe.

As we neared our destination, the paved roads turned to gravel roads. There wasn't much to see but muddy, hilly terrain dotted with huts, and shacks lining the side of the road with signs advertising wood coffins for sale.

I saw boys that looked no more than ten or eleven years old laboring at the side of the road, busily hammering together wooden body boxes. Suzanne had stopped talking. We both just stared out of the car window at those boys building coffins.

We met up with a local relief worker and spent the morning delivering fifty-pound bags of cornmeal to families. Along the way, we connected with several African women who worked as caregivers. The relief worker explained that so many people were sick and dying that these women were paid the equivalent of thirty dollars a month to make the rounds to patients. She said the caregivers washed and comforted their patients, brought them food, tried to ease their pain and nausea and, in many cases, offered dying parents the assurance that their children would be looked after when they were gone.

"The only problem is that there are so many orphans it is impossible for these women to care for all of the children being left behind," the relief worker explained. "And on top of that, many of these women are probably HIV-positive themselves. We don't know the true percentage of HIV cases because many people are too scared to get tested."

After wrapping up our morning food deliveries, Suzanne and I decided to spend the afternoon accompanying a caregiver on some of her patient visits. We parked our car along a muddy slope and followed Thandi, a woman in her mid-forties, through a muddy weed path to visit with dying men and women who lay on cots in the tiny cement huts that cluttered the area. Sometimes Thandi just stroked the dying person's hand or put a cool cloth on his or her forehead. Other times, she spoon-fed them some cornmeal mush or gave them some herbs to help with nausea. One hut after the next, it was the same horrific scene: a person wasting away on a small, dirty cot while suffering through unbearable heat, the stench of human waste, and endless swarms of flies. It was hard to tell how old these sick and dying people were because their bodies were so emaciated. But I guessed that most of them were my age or younger.

Every part of me wanted to wave a magic wand and fix this. And if I couldn't, I at least wanted to get out of there. It was too overwhelming, too horrible, too hopeless.

"There is someone special I want you to meet," Thandi said after wrapping up our sixth or seventh patient visit.

I wasn't sure what to expect as Suzanne and I followed Thandi through another quarter-mile of weeds and mud. All I could think about was how much strength it must take to wake up every day and endure the misery of watching these people suffer and die without having any way to save them.

Thandi stopped in front of a hut where two young boys and a girl were busy pulling weeds. The oldest and clear leader of the group was the girl, who Thandi introduced as Nathanda. She was thin and pretty and wore a faded red cotton dress. Despite the mud and weeds, I noticed that her feet were bare.

Nathanda looked up at us, nodded, and then went back to weeding. While we watched the kids work, Thandi told us that Nathanda, who was eleven, had lost both of her parents to AIDS a few months earlier—leaving her the sole caretaker for her two younger brothers, ages eight and five.

"She was living in the hut with her brothers, caring for them and surviving on donated bags of cornmeal," Thandi started out, shaking her head. "One night a couple of weeks ago, she went to a neighboring hut to borrow an iron so she could press her school uniform—which is necessary to kill the maggot eggs that get into the clothes. A man followed her back to her hut and raped her while her little brothers watched."

Raped? Eleven years old? While her brothers watched?

I locked my eyes on Nathanda, willing my brain to comprehend the enormity of being eleven years old, orphaned, and left to care for two little boys. It wasn't just that Nathanda had to watch over them. She had to figure out how to get the food to keep them alive and make sure they had clothes to wear and a place to sleep. She had to comfort them when they cried out for their parents—with no one to care for and comfort her. The idea that amid all of this, a man would invade the safety of her little hut and rape her was too much for my brain to process.

"She is one of the lucky ones," Thandi continued quietly. "She had an HIV test and it turned out negative. But now her hut is starting to crumble, making it unsafe for her and her brothers to stay here. So at night, Nathanda and her brothers sleep on my floor. But during the day, she stands guard over her hut to make sure squatters don't take over."

HIV? It didn't even occur to me until Thandi said it that the rape could have meant a death sentence for Nathanda. The fact that Thandi used the word "lucky" to describe Nathanda's situation was too much.

Thandi stopped talking and everything went silent. Nathanda had noticed my eyes locked on her and was now looking intently back at me. There was so much pain in those big black-brown eyes. Though no one was speaking, Thandi's words and their dire meaning were screams in my mind: both parents dead within months of each other. Nathanda left on her own to care for her brothers. No one to protect her from the rapists and thugs. And now homeless.

How could this be her life? How could so much awfulness be heaped on one young girl?

Without saying a word, Nathanda stepped closer to me, took my hand, and led me into her cement hut. It was just one room—maybe a hundred square feet. A double bed and a twin bed that were both pushed against the back wall took up most of the room. The worn bedspreads covering each mattress were carefully made. A beat-up teddy bear sat propped up against a pillow.

I felt Nathanda tugging on my hand. She pointed to the shelf on the opposite wall. It was lined with cornmeal and a few cups and plates that had been neatly arranged. Underneath that was another shelf that contained a few carefully folded shirts and pants.

"Very nice," I said, hoping the smile I forced on my face hid the horror I was feeling. "You are a very good housekeeper and I can tell you do a great job taking care of your brothers."

Nathanda looked at me, confused. Thandi, who had followed us into the hut, quickly translated my words into Swahili.

I don't know why it didn't occur to me that this little girl didn't speak English. Why I thought she had time to learn a foreign language.

I looked at Thandi for help.

"Can you ask her what she would wish for if she could have any wish?"

I'm not sure why I asked this. I just felt so helpless and needed to know that she still dreamed and still had hope for the future.

Thandi nodded and rattled off my question to Nathanda.

For a minute, Nathanda didn't speak. I watched the tears puddle in her eyes and spill onto her cheeks. Then she said something to Thandi.

"She says that she would like someone to fix her house so she and her brothers can move back in," Thandi translated, motioning to the long vertical crack running down the cement wall behind the beds. "And she says, 'One day, I hope I can be happy'."

Thandi kept her face steady but her voice cracked when she translated this last line. My arms wrapped around Nathanda.

I wanted to tell her it would be okay—that my stories would inspire people to donate money to help make life better for her. Even more, I wanted to take her home with me to live so I could show her what happiness felt like.

I reached in my bag and pulled out some Starburst candies, along with a self-portrait that my five-year-old daughter, Syd had drawn. That's what I had to offer this little girl who had lost so much: a crayon drawing of a smiling brown-haired girl and a handful of candy.

As we retraced our steps through the muddy pathways back to our car, Thandi told us that Nathanda and her brothers were now among a group of fifteen orphans who slept on the floor in her two-room hut each night.

"I'm doing my best to look after her and the others and keep them safe. But it's hard and I don't know how much longer I can do it."

Now my eyes were locked on Thandi's stoic face, which looked like it couldn't hold up much longer. "I've got six children of my own. And I just tested positive for HIV."

Suzanne and I didn't talk when we climbed back into the car. Neither of us could find the words.

As previously arranged, we reconnected with the relief worker we'd met earlier in the day. She was also making the rounds to visit the sick and dying and told us she had one last stop to make. We drove along a gravel road until it ended and then followed the relief worker on foot up a hill and through a broken barbed-wire fence. The temperature now topped 110 degrees and my T-shirt was soaked with sweat. As we neared the hut, the familiar stench of human waste filled the air—only it was a lot stronger than anything I had encountered so far that day. Seated in the scorching sun about ten yards in front of the hut was a tall, thin girl—nineteen years old according to the relief worker. A little boy, who looked to be around two—the same age as my Hannah—stood next to her.

As we walked closer to the girl, I noticed that she was sitting on what appeared to be a white plastic sheet. She stared straight ahead, oblivious to our presence. On the other side of her lay a baby wrapped in a dirty blanket. The baby wasn't moving or making a sound.

My eyes went from the baby back to the girl and the white plastic sheet.

"What *is* that?" I asked the relief worker, swatting away at the flies buzzing in my face.

"That's a body bag—it's one distributed by our organization," she answered quietly. "She's waiting to die."

A body bag? She was sitting on her own body bag?

"What are you talking about?" I snapped. "Where is her family? Why isn't she being cared for? Why isn't anyone helping her with her kids? Where is everyone?"

I looked at the little boy, who wore only a T-shirt, no bottoms. He was clinging to his mom's shoulder and staring at us with big, fearful eyes. His mouth was turned in a quivering frown, like he was ready to cry. Flies crawled on his check and near his mouth, but he didn't make a move to swat them away.

"He's HIV-positive too," the relief worker whispered.

I felt my gut drop into my stomach. Homesickness washed over me. All I could think of was Hannah—my chubby, happy, healthy toddler—probably asleep in her crib at the moment. I wanted to be there at home with her, holding her. Not here in the suffocating heat and stench, looking at this little boy who would soon be dead.

While Suzanne and I stood frozen and helpless, the relief worker went to work. She picked up the baby, which we later learned was a girl. We heard her make a small noise. The baby, for now, was still alive.

"We've got to get them some food," the relief worker said. "Let's see if there's something in the hut."

I trailed behind her to the entryway of the hut, where the smell was so overpowering I tried not to breathe. On the dirt floor was a pile of soiled clothes and in one corner was a half-eaten tin cup of cornmeal mush, covered in flies.

The relief worker grabbed the tin cup, dumped out the old mush, wiped it down with a corner of her T-shirt, and filled it with fresh cornmeal and water from her water bottle.

She returned to the boy, who was still clinging to his mother's shoulder, and knelt beside him.

"Here," she said gently, trying to spoon-feed him the cornmeal. He pushed her hand away and shook his head.

"Here," she said more forcefully, trying to force the spoon into his mouth. "You need to eat."

The toddler let the food get into his mouth, but immediately spit it out. It was hard to tell if he was too scared to eat, or if he was too sick to be hungry.

After a few minutes, the relief worker gave up. She picked up the baby, cradled her, and sprinkled water drops into her mouth.

"I've got to get some help here," the relief worker said finally, dialing a number on the field phone she held. "We've got to do something about this."

Three hours later, I was sitting on the tiled veranda at a nearby wild game resort, enjoying an African barbeque while I watched giraffes graze in the distance. It was the only place in the vicinity with housing and the owners of the resort had provided the rooms at huge discounts. But it was impossible not to feel guilty for enjoying the lavish comforts of a four-star resort while Nathanda guarded her dilapidated hut from squatters and the nineteen-year-old girl, her baby, and her two-year-old son baked in the heat while they waited to die.

Suzanne and I had encountered so much suffering and dying throughout the day that it had been a relief to be able to hop in the car and drive away from it all. As soon as we had arrived at the lodge and checked into our rooms, I was in the shower washing away the sweat and dirt caked on my body. The cool water and soap had been such a welcome relief and escape. But I couldn't wash away the fact that no one living in that muddy, sweltering, desolate village only thirty miles from where I was now could escape it with us. They couldn't just dabble in it for a day and declare that they'd had enough. They couldn't hop in a car and drive away from the stench of dying people, the sickness, the starvation, the despair that surrounded them. They had no clean air-conditioned room waiting for them. There was no bathroom equipped with a shower and soap to wash away the grime caked on their bodies. They didn't even have the luxury of running water or a toilet. The vast majority of the people living there would probably never even know a place like this resort existed.

"Look at that sunset," I heard one of our hosts say. "Isn't that beautiful?"

I let my eyes once again sweep the immense Saharan landscape with the giraffes and pink-golden sun retreating in the distance. For the first time since my eye diagnosis, I noticed what I could see instead of what I was missing out on. I could see everything I looked at—in rich, vibrant colors.

I felt my gut tighten.

What did I have to be upset about? I had everything—two amazing, healthy daughters and a husband who loved me. I would soon be moving into a new house in a neighborhood where I could walk or bus everywhere I wanted or needed to go. I had great friends. I had a great job. And though John and I sometimes struggled financially, we'd never had to worry about going without food or shelter.

I hadn't been given a death sentence. I had been diagnosed with a slowly progressing degenerative eye disease. It wasn't even for certain that I would go completely blind.

As I sipped the crisp cold Chardonnay that had just been handed to me by our hosts, I made a vow to myself: whatever was going to happen with my eyesight, I was done feeling sorry for myself.

5

FOUR YEARS LATER - EARLY 2008

I<small>T STARTED WITH</small> an email from a friend. For the past two years, we had been sharing carpooling duties for our two daughters and I was trying to coordinate schedules for the upcoming week.

"No offense, but I don't want you driving my daughter anymore," his email read. "I just can't risk it, if you know what I mean."

I felt like I had been sucker punched. For a minute, I just stared at the note, too stunned to respond. Once my brain unfroze enough to think, I was so angry and hurt I considered showing up at his door and clawing his eyes out.

I had dared share my secret with this person who I thought was my friend. And this is what I got in return?

Since moving to Seattle four years earlier, I had been careful to guard my eye condition and had only told a few close friends. I didn't want people pitying me or looking down on me. But what I feared most was being discriminated against—especially when I felt like I had everything under control.

The Africa trip had snapped me out of my depression and made me realize how fortunate I was to be dealing with a slow moving eye disease rather than a devastating terminal illness such as AIDS. But now that I was out of the dark fog, I was back to my regular action- and control-oriented self.

After what I had seen and experienced in Africa, it felt wrong to mourn my vision loss. So instead, I did the next best thing— convince myself that it would all just go away if I took charge of the situation and made a few modifications to my lifestyle.

Looking back now, I can see that I was engaged in some serious denial. But even at that, I did feel like I had grounds for hope. Despite the doomed prognosis from the retinal specialist, he had also said something that made me believe there was more to the disease than just a faulty gene. He had been talking about the challenge of projecting how fast RP would advance in a given person—due to the fact that there were a variety of genes that had been linked to RP. But then he mentioned environmental factors.

"You could have identical twins separated at birth and the disease could track completely different in each of them," he'd said.

This, to me, confirmed that external factors such as nutrition could make a difference in the rate of progression even if the retinal specialist didn't believe there was a correlation. Once back in Seattle, I immediately began formulating my own eye health program that I convinced myself would halt the progression of the disease. I started pumping my body full of every eye-focused nutritional supplement I could get my hands on and changed my diet to include plenty of leafy greens. And it seemed to be working. A trip back to the retinal specialist a year after my diagnosis had found my peripheral vision holding steady. What's more, my central vision had actually improved to 20/15.

I thought I heard surprise in the doctor's voice and it made me feel victorious.

"So is it possible that my eyesight could stay this way for the rest of my life?" I asked him, trying not to gloat.

"Sure—it's possible," he replied. He even smiled a little when he said it and I concluded that maybe he wasn't such a bad guy after all.

I began viewing my eye disease as a wake-up call that had scared me into action and enabled me to make the necessary changes to get my health back on track and preserve my remaining vision. Like everything else in my life, I felt like I had my RP under control. And the bonus was that I now got to live in Seattle.

Once settled into my new neighborhood, I had refrained from driving on freeways or busy roads. I had also stopped driving after dusk when my night vision problems kicked in. But I figured I was still fine driving the quiet streets throughout my neighborhood and had been doing it without a problem for the past four years.

Driving gave me a sense of freedom. But I also didn't feel like I had much of a choice. With John logging as many as sixty hours a week at his firm, the responsibility of shuttling Syd and Hannah to their dance, art and sports activities fell on me.

Because of my eye disease, I was an exceptionally careful driver and as far as I could tell, it was all working out fine. The idea that one of the few people I had entrusted with my secret suddenly felt he needed to protect his daughter from *me* was infuriating. And devastating. I felt like my integrity was being questioned and that a piece of me was being ripped away. His words were razors—each one cutting deep into my self-esteem.

"Do whatever you want to do," I shot back in my own email. "But I would NEVER drive if I thought I was putting anyone at risk. I wouldn't do that. You should know that."

Amid my rage and hurt, it didn't occur to me how difficult it must have been for my friend to broach such a sensitive subject. I also didn't realize that by focusing all of my anger on him, I was essentially punishing him for daring to be the messenger. Looking back now and putting myself in his shoes, I can see how absurd I was being. Of course he didn't want a legally blind person driving his daughter, regardless of the status of our friendship (though I still would have preferred the message delivered in person over tequila shots). But at the time, all I could concentrate on was the pain charging through me—pain that his words had caused.

I doubled my resolve to hide my eye condition from everyone around me. The only way people could hurt me was if they knew, and I wasn't going to give anyone else that kind of power over me. But deep down, I was scared. Because the truth that I had been guarding even from myself was that my eyesight was slipping. I had been sensing it closing in on me for the past few months but I had refused to acknowledge it. I kept hoping it was all in my head.

A few weeks after receiving that painful email, I accompanied John, Syd, and Hannah to our local coffee shop for our Saturday morning tradition of bagels and coffee. Amid the crowd, I didn't see the hundred-pound Golden Retriever that had settled into a spot on the main pathway.

I headed to the counter to grab a plate with my bagel and cream cheese. I rounded the corner slowly, carefully navigating the obstacle course of people, tables, and chairs that separated me from the other side of the room where my family was seated.

I felt my foot and knee catch on something furry. Then I felt my body slamming against the cement floor, caught only by a furry lump that was suddenly barking and yelping.

"Are you okay?" I heard an anxious woman ask behind me. I pulled myself up to see her hugging her dog and shooting me what I interpreted as a "you are a disgusting human being" look.

"Sorry," I mumbled as I pushed myself to my feet.

I felt a hundred accusing eyes on me as Syd rushed to my side. A barista materialized from behind the counter and fetched my broken plate and bagel from the ground.

"Would you like me to make you another one?" she asked, trying to keep her tone patient.

"No. I'm not hungry anymore," I snapped, following Syd to the table where John and Hannah sat.

I was burning with humiliation. Who wanted to see a forty-one-year-old woman do a belly flop over a dog? I could hear the criticism in people's minds, wondering why I hadn't been more careful and watched where I was going.

"Don't worry about it," John said, reaching across the table to squeeze my hand. "The dog shouldn't have been there in the first place. That woman can go screw herself."

I nodded my head and tried to mentally pull myself together. I couldn't tell John what I was terrified to acknowledge myself: that despite my all-out efforts to control it, my eyesight was getting worse.

That evening I filled a large water glass with wine, climbed into the claw-foot tub in our recently remodeled basement bathroom, turned off the lights, and let myself go. I tried to keep my sobs silent because I didn't want John or the girls to hear me. I didn't want to alarm them. But even more, I didn't want to have to explain. I wasn't sure I was even capable of finding the words to voice the terror and pain I was feeling.

John must have sensed something was wrong because after a few minutes, I heard a knock on the glass slider door.

"Is everything all right?"

His voice sounded concerned and when I didn't answer, I heard the slider door open and then shut behind him. Then he was kneeling beside the tub.

"What's going on? What's wrong?"

For a few minutes I could only shake my head and let the tears slide down my face. I wasn't sure if I could say the words out loud. Saying them made them real.

"It's getting worse," I finally blurted. "A lot worse. What if I really go blind?"

John was quiet for a minute.

"Then we'll figure it out," he said.

"How? How are we going to do that?" I sobbed, trying not to sound hysterical. "What if I can't see you or the girls? How am I going to work or get by or help out? And what about you? How are you going to deal with it if I'm blind? Why would you want a blind wife?"

There. I had voiced them. The questions that had been swirling in my mind since my diagnosis. The questions that I had been too scared to say out loud. I braced myself, ready for John to deliver the final blow.

He stayed quiet for another minute. But he continued to hold my hand.

"So you go blind. We'll deal with it," he said finally. "It's not like someone has given you a death sentence or taken away your brain. You can still think, right? We'll be fine. I'm not going anywhere."

He seemed so calm and matter of fact. More than that, he sounded genuine and convincing—like having a blind wife wasn't the end of the world. The way he made it sound, going blind was like having a bad cough or something. Of course, I don't know what else he would have said in that situation. But still it was comforting to hear that he wasn't ready to pack his bags yet.

But now that we were having the conversation, I couldn't stop.

"But what about work? How am I going to work? And what about my book and getting back to my personal writing? What if I run out of time and I'm still doing my client work?"

After writing the stories about the plight of AIDS orphans for the African Children's Choir, I had resumed the marketing communications work I'd been doing ever since John had graduated from law school. My original plan had been to work at the ad agency while John was in law school, and then—as soon as he graduated—return to the social-issues journalism and other personal writing I loved. I especially wanted to write books and had been slowly plowing away at my own coming-of-age story. But then the kids came along and bills piled up. We were always just barely getting by financially and it only seemed to be getting worse.

John had recently been made a partner at his small law firm. While it sounded good, it meant that he now got paid only when clients paid, instead of being paid monthly for the work he had billed. But because he wasn't the primary attorney on the biggest accounts he worked on, he wasn't allowed to contact clients when invoices became overdue. On top of that, he was now responsible for covering a portion of the firm's huge overhead each month. Despite his working twelve-hour days at least six days a week, we weren't getting ahead. Most months, he wasn't even able to bring home a paycheck.

"Then write your book and quit your client work. We'll be fine."

John was saying all the right words. But my mind was rejecting them.

Right. How could I just quit my client work and focus on personal writing when my client income was the only thing keeping us afloat? I knew John was just trying to help, just trying to make me feel better and fix the situation. But my mind told me it wasn't realistic. And even if it was doable, there was a bigger issue I was dealing with: trust.

A few months earlier—during one of our now rare conversations given that he was always gone so much—John and I had talked about taking risks.

"You know what your biggest risk would be?" he had said quietly. "Allowing yourself to depend on me."

At the time, I hadn't even known how to respond. Growing up, I had learned the hard way that the only person I could count on was myself. Depending on others just meant a lot of pain and hurt. I wanted to lean on John. I just didn't know how to do it and didn't trust it. And given the constant financial stress we were under, I couldn't imagine how cutting back on my client work and going after my writing dream was ever going to be a possibility— regardless of John's encouragement.

"I guess the first thing to do is get your eyes checked so we know where we stand," John said, interrupting my thoughts.

I hadn't seen the retinal specialist since three years before, when the news was good. Now, knowing my vision had taken a turn for the worse, I was scared of what the tests would show. But John was right. We needed to know what we were dealing with.

The next day I worked up the nerve to schedule an appointment for an eye exam and visual field test. The minute I stared into that now familiar visual field box, I knew my fears were confirmed. Unless the dot flashed directly in front of me, I couldn't see it. But in my far outer periphery, it was a different matter. Though I couldn't see the fine dots, I could pick up the bigger flashes of light, including in places that I didn't remember seeing them before.

"Well. It's tracking like we expected it would," the retinal specialist announced when he walked into the patient room with my test results a few minutes later. "Your visual field has definitely closed in on you."

His words stung.

"What do you mean?" I shot back. "I thought you said last time that there was a chance it wouldn't get any worse."

"Well there is always a chance," he replied. "But that's not how I've ever seen it work with this disease."

I felt my body get shaky but I took a deep breath, determined to keep myself calm.

"But what about the expanded blurry vision in my far periphery?" I asked. "I mean, that's pretty significant, right? If it's getting better out there, doesn't that mean there's hope that this could get better all the way around?"

The retinal specialist wore the same stern, deadpan face I remembered from the first visit.

"We don't know why that happens at times, but it is part of the way this disease tracks. It doesn't mean anything in terms of your overall prognosis. I'm sorry."

I left his office vowing never to go back again. What was the point of going to a doctor who couldn't help me?

I went home and started another intense Google search on possible treatments and cures for Retinitis Pigmentosa. Regardless of the fact that the retinal specialist had dismissed it, I couldn't let go of the only hope I now had to hold onto: that the thin strip of vision in my far periphery had expanded. True, it was blurry. And it had appeared at the same time that my sharp central vision had shrunk from ten to around five degrees. But however blurry, I could now make out large shapes in my outer periphery in places that were blank before. That had to be a positive. It had to mean that there was a way to reverse this disease. There had to be some answers out there somewhere. There had to be someone who could help me.

Combing through a couple of RP chat boards, I came across the name of a Dr. Damon Miller in northern California who treated serious eye disorders. In searching his name, I located his Web site. What I read fascinated me. Dr. Miller was trained as an MD, but had added naturopathic medicine after watching patients become dependent on pharmaceutical drugs and seeing the adverse side affects.

For years he had been working with serious degenerative eye diseases that Western Medicine said were non-curable. Through an intensive home treatment program that included nutritional supplements, eye exercises, acupressure, stress management, color lamp therapy, and something called micro-current stimulation— in which small doses of electrical currents were pumped into a patient's eye—he claimed to be halting the progression of RP and macular degeneration.

The next morning I called his office and scheduled a phone consultation. I had so many questions, and unlike the retinal specialist, he sounded like someone who might be able to answer them for me.

One big question that had been nagging me since my diagnosis was the cause of the disease. Everything I had read online and heard from the retinal specialist indicated that RP was a hereditary disease that could result from one of numerous faulty genes. Yet I hadn't been able to find one relative in my extended family who suffered from RP. My mom's relatives were scattered throughout Europe and there was always the possibility that someone, somewhere suffered from it. But my mom was connected with most of them and no one she knew had anything like this.

I kept thinking back to a car accident I'd been in when I was twelve. I was seated in the front passenger seat when a car plowed into my door going forty miles per hour. I had been pinned under a mass of metal and glass from the passenger window that had shattered across the right side of my face and head.

No medical tests were performed to determine what kind of head injury might have occurred. But I'd had more than a hundred stitches in the right side of my forehead and sustained so much nerve damage that nearly thirty years later, even small bumps to that area on my forehead caused the entire right half of my head to throb in excruciating pain and tingle like hitting my funny bone.

Was it possible that my RP was the result of my head injury? And if so, did that mean there was a way to fix it? I rattled off my head injury theory as soon as I got on the phone with Dr. Miller, but he immediately dismissed it.

"I've not heard of that correlation before," he replied. "But let me ask you this. Have you experienced any severe emotional trauma in your life where you've seen something that you just couldn't bear to see because it was so stressful and traumatic?"

His question surprised me. What did emotional trauma have to do with my eyesight? I was leery of anything touchy feely that suggested bad childhoods were the root of adult problems. It sounded like an excuse for people who were too weak to take responsibility for their own lives. I had always been a deal-with-it-yourself kind of person. But before I had time to put voice to these thoughts, my mind flashed back to an early July morning the summer after I had turned sixteen. My dad, an independent traveling salesman, had become my escape from an unbearable home life and an abusive stepdad I hated. Whenever I wasn't in school, I was with my dad—living on the road selling tools.

That early July morning we were on a freeway in Illinois—on our way to a meeting in Wisconsin—and had just been pulled over for speeding. I assumed the highway patrolman was in his car writing up a speeding ticket. I couldn't figure out why my dad looked so nervous, and why his eyes kept darting to the rearview mirror.

"Oh shit!" he suddenly yelled.

Before I could respond, I heard the patrolman screaming for us to put our hands in the air and keep them where he could see them. Then I saw the gun, inches from my dad's head.

I watched in horror as the patrolman dragged my dad out of our car with one hand while keeping his gun trained on my dad's head. My arms and hands stayed frozen in the air while my eyes locked on the image I would never forget: the patrolman slamming my dad against the back of our car, shoving handcuffs on him, and taking him away from me. My dad, my safety net— the one person in the world who kept me going when I thought I couldn't survive another day at home—was gone. Even thinking about it all these years later made me shake a little.

My thoughts switched back to the room and the phone receiver in my hand.

"Yeah," I replied softly into the phone. "I can think of an instance."

Dr. Miller was quiet for a minute. "Well, I have seen a correlation between RP and intense emotional trauma."

So he was telling me that a serious physical head injury couldn't be related to my eye problems but some emotional trauma that happened back when I was a teenager could?

It sounded bizarre and a little far-fetched. But Dr. Miller didn't come across as a quack. He sounded calm, knowledgeable, and matter of fact. I asked Dr. Miller about the expanded blurry vision in my outer periphery. He didn't have a concrete reason for why that had occurred at the same time my sharp central vision had shrunk, but he stressed his belief that the body could heal itself if it was given the nutrition and other tools it needed. Our conversation continued on to Dr. Miller's treatment program. He talked about taking a whole body approach that looked at both emotional and physical health. He stressed the critical importance of nutrition and stress management. He also discussed the combination of alternative therapies he used—which included micro-current stimulation where small doses of electrical current were applied to the eyes to stimulate cells and blood flow and help rid the cells of toxins.

Though naturopathy was completely foreign to me, Dr. Miller's words resonated with me. And the fact that he was also a Board-certified MD made me feel a little more comfortable about exploring the alternative treatment he offered.

By the time I hung up the phone, I knew I wanted to start on his home treatment program, which he explained was a lifestyle commitment that required extensive daily work by the patient. But beyond that, I knew I needed to meet him in person to go through his detoxification program and learn more about his whole body approach to health.

As soon as I hung up the phone with Dr. Miller, I called John and told him I wanted to go to California to visit this guy. I told him about his alternative treatments but purposefully left out the part about my eye disease possibly being related to emotional stress. I knew he would have a harder time swallowing that than I did.

John was hesitant but supportive. "It's up to you," he said. "It's a lot of money and you know our financial situation. But if that's what you want to do and think there is a chance it could help, go for it."

Dr. Miller's detoxification and treatment program took four days and there was no way John could afford to take time off from work to be with the kids—even a day off meant getting further in debt to his firm.

For one of the first times in my life, I called my mom in Utah and asked her for help.

"Can I fly you up to Seattle to watch the girls for a few days while John's at work?" I asked. "I need to go to California and see a doctor about my eyes. And I want to do it as soon as possible."

6

I LIKED DR. MILLER the instant I met him. He was about six feet tall, with a receding hairline and warm brown eyes that were as soft and welcoming as his voice. I guessed that he was in his late forties or early fifties, though he looked so fit and healthy his body age was probably only around thirty.

Unlike the retinal specialist's office, which was located in a hospital and made me feel sick just walking into it, Dr. Miller's office was somewhere between a yoga studio and meditation retreat center. The floors were covered in terracotta tile and bamboo, accented with beautiful multi-colored rugs and rattan furniture. The walls were painted in warm yellows with a sky-blue ceiling, and soothing instrumental music played in the background.

After greeting me personally in the waiting area, Dr. Miller escorted me into a small room with a patient table and two chairs facing each other. He motioned for me to sit in one of them and then took a seat across from me, so close that my knees were only inches from his.

"So tell me about the day you were born," he said, looking directly into my eyes.

I should have guessed based on our phone conversation that there was a possibility that personal questions would arise. But it still surprised me. It seemed strange to just start divulging such personal information about myself. Yet there was something about his calm, straightforward manner—combined with the fact that I had just spent the time and money to fly to California to meet him in person—that made me decide to go along with it.

"Okay," I replied, trying not to sound as hesitant as I felt. "If you really want to hear it."

As soon as I started talking, I felt my voice quiver and I could feel the blood rushing to my face. I had no idea where this sudden flood of emotion was coming from. I chalked it up to nerves.

I recounted the story I had heard in bits and pieces from both of my parents about the day I was born: the two of them flat-broke and stuck in Ohio in a tiny dark apartment—with a three-year-old daughter and a marriage already strained from ongoing financial stress and constant head-butting.

The way my dad always told it, my mom was in hard labor with me by the time he found a hospital willing to admit her despite their lack of money and health insurance. He rushed her by car to the emergency room entrance, where she was whisked away by wheelchair to the delivery room. Almost immediately, my dad said a hospital administrator began hounding him for payment, even though he made it clear he didn't have a penny to his name. It didn't take long for him to explode.

For some reason, just hearing him tell the story would always send my stress levels through the roof.

"Now I just want you to picture this, Ingrid," my dad would say to me, laughing as he recounted the memory. "I just go crazy.

I start running down that hospital hall and I'm screaming at the top of my lungs, `WHERE IS MY WIFE! I WANT MY WIFE OUT OF HERE. NOW!' I was like a mad man, I was so out of control. Well, now I've definitely got their attention but I'm so angry I can't even see straight. I just keep screaming and hitting the walls, demanding that they get my wife out of there. Well of course it's too late because at that very moment, you were being born but I didn't know that at the time."

My dad told me that the same administrator who had been badgering him prior to his explosion was now trailing behind him, begging him to stop for the sake of the patients. The man was so desperate for my dad to stop that he offered to arrange whatever payment terms were needed. Eventually my dad calmed down enough to work out a five dollar a month payment plan to cover my birth.

I finished my story and looked up at Dr. Miller.

"Keep going. Tell me about your childhood," he prodded.

Soon I was detailing a rocky, painful childhood with a volatile, free-spirited dad who dealt with his unhappy marriage by leaving us for months at a time, engaging in extramarital affairs and rarely sending enough money to support us, and an emotionally battered mother who, unable to depend on her husband, had turned over her life—and ours—to religion as a coping mechanism.

When I got to the part about my parents' divorce and my mom's marriage six months later to a man who exploited the religious powers he had been given to abuse and oppress our family, I lost it.

I was suddenly sobbing so hard it was a struggle to breathe. I didn't know where it was coming from, but once the tears started, I couldn't stop. It was like years of pain and hurt buried deep inside just started unraveling. I sat in that chair sobbing—huge racking sobs I didn't know I was even capable of.

Dr. Miller grabbed a box of tissues and handed them to me. Then he sat quietly, listening as the sobs and anguish came.

Finally, after about five minutes, I was able to regain enough composure to talk. I was so humiliated by my breakdown I couldn't even look at him. What was wrong with me?

"Sorry about that," I mumbled, staring at the floor. "Don't know where that came from."

Dr. Miller stopped me.

"There is nothing to be sorry for," he said kindly. "Addressing your emotional health is part of the reason you are here. But one thing is really clear to me. You are carrying a huge negative energy charge inside you over something that happened years ago."

He paused for a minute to let his words sink in. I'd never thought of emotions as an energy source or drain carried around inside me. I'd heard stories about emotional baggage but I really thought I had escaped my past. Once I had been able to get out on my own, I had set my sights on my future and never looked back. And until my eye diagnosis, I thought I'd been doing well.

I felt Dr. Miller looking at me intently. His next words were in the same quiet voice but his intensity had changed. "Do you realize that carrying this kind of hurt and stress inside of you is having a serious impact on your physical health? And do you realize how much of your power you are giving to those people who hurt you all those years ago? The thing about it is, you're giving it to them and they probably don't even realize it."

His words, which had started as a slow drizzle, were now pelting me. I sat in my chair, feeling them first hit me—and then penetrate me.

I had never thought about it like that before. Actually I'd never thought about it at all. But I knew he was right. I was a forty-one-year-old woman who still found myself overcome with rage every time I thought about the stepdad who had taken my power and voice from me as a teenager. I hadn't seen him in years. But just hearing his name, even if it belonged to someone else, made me shake with emotion. I felt the same anger when I thought of my mom. I knew she was a good person. And we had all moved on with our lives. Yet I couldn't let go of the fact that she had married that man—brought him into our home—and then let him hurt my siblings and me. My dad had always been absent. But it was my mom I was angry with. Now that I had daughters of my own, it seemed inconceivable to me that a mother could stand by and allow someone to hurt her children.

I jumped from that thought to Dr. Miller's comment about my emotional baggage affecting my physical health. Could it be true that I was letting the hurt and pain from all those years ago steal my vision?

"So if my emotions are making me sick, how do I get rid of them?" I asked him blankly.

Dr. Miller probably wished he had never agreed to an in-person treatment with me. I don't know how he remained so calm. Encountering a blubbering mess like myself would have driven me crazy.

"I think it starts with consciously recognizing it," he said simply.

My treatment over the four days of appointments with Dr. Miller contained various detoxification procedures (including probiotics designed to clean out a person's intestines), nutritional counseling, lessons in acupressure and eye exercises, color lamp therapy—in which colored screens are used to stimulate the eyes, and overall stress management techniques.

It also included learning how to properly use the MicroStim device that was at the core of the extensive daily treatment program I would be self-administering at home.

The MicroStim unit was a small battery-operated rectangular gadget the size of a point-and-shoot pocket camera. The device was attached to wires that in turn were attached to two black eye pads and a Velcro headband.

Dr. Miller demonstrated it for me, first putting wet cotton balls on the eye pads and then attaching the Velcro band around his head so the cotton ball-lined eye pads rested on his eyes.

"Just turn the knob like this and then adjust it as necessary until you feel gentle pulses in your eyes," he explained, twisting the small knob on the device while wearing the gear like a blindfold. "Just make sure you don't feel it in your teeth. If you do, it's on too high."

The idea of pumping electrical currents into my eyes freaked me out a little. But it also intrigued me. Dr. Miller's explanation was so logical and easy to follow that it made a lot of sense to me. He talked about waste building up in the eye cells, which in turn kept the cells from absorbing the necessary nutrients to thrive. He said micro-current stimulation—which was commonly used in sports medication to speed the healing process of torn tissue—helped boost the cells' abilities to rid themselves of waste products. He said it also increased blood supply to the stimulated area, providing eye cells with additional oxygen and nourishment.

"It won't electrocute me, right?" I asked before following his lead and trying it out for myself.

I was mostly joking but Dr. Miller didn't find it funny.

"Nothing we ever do here causes harm or pain," he said sternly. "We are focused on healing, not harming."

Once I got the hang of the micro-current stimulation device and learned how to identify acupressure points on my face, arms, hands, and feet to further stimulate blood supply and eliminate toxins from my body, Dr. Miller got down to the business of every day stress management.

"So what do you do to manage your stress?" he asked. "Do you get regular body massages?"

I laughed, imagining the luxury of spending the time and money on weekly body massages.

"No. But does alcohol count?"

Dr. Miller's mouth turned down into a frown. "Well, you should be getting regular massages. Think of your body like a car. It requires regular maintenance or it breaks down.

"You shouldn't be drinking alcohol," he added. "It's a toxin to your central nervous system, which directly affects your eyes."

Maybe he saw the devastated look on my face because he quickly modified his last statement.

"If it was me, I wouldn't drink at all. But maybe for you, drinking one or two glasses of wine a week isn't a bad thing if it acts as a stress reliever, because I can tell that stress is a serious problem for you. But just make sure you keep it to a couple of glasses a week. And work on ways to reduce that stress because it's horrible for your health."

I breathed a sigh of relief. I wasn't ready to give up wine. Sometimes it was the only thing getting me through the week. But I did make a mental note to myself: cut down on drinking and work on stress reduction.

Along with everything else, Dr. Miller continued to delve deeper into my family history. He asked me about my mom and her mom. Sometimes, he would also ask about my relationship with John and our family situation at home.

He said the reason for his probing personal questions had to do with the relatively new, evolving medical field of epigenetics, which focuses on the environmental factors such as diet and lifestyle that determine when a gene is expressed, and when it remains dormant.

"You've been told this is a genetic disease, but the questions to ask are, 'Why is it showing up now when you are so much older? Why didn't you start having troubles with your eyes when you were a child?' You've had this abnormal gene from birth."

Dr. Miller referred to the identical twin research that the retinal specialist had mentioned—that you could have identical twins with the same genetic markers yet one would get the disease, the other wouldn't. But now I had a concrete explanation for why this occurred. And I understood now that it wasn't just lack of nutrition that could activate a disease. Emotional trauma or even physical trauma that wore down a person's overall health could change a gene's reaction. It made a lot of sense, as did Dr. Miller's explanation behind his comprehensive treatment program: that if you could get the body back to the level of health it once had, it could begin to heal itself.

As part of my four-day treatment program with Dr. Miller, I had to refrain from using my computer or cell phone. Given that my marketing communications business revolved around those two devices, it took some serious willpower to stay clear of them both. But in doing so, I found myself with hours of unoccupied time to think. And I had been doing lots of it. I couldn't get over what Dr. Miller had said about the role emotional trauma had played in my eye disease. Or the fact that I had been devoting so much of my unconscious energy to feeling hurt and angry over the pain my stepdad had caused me more than twenty years earlier. The more I thought about it, the more ludicrous the notion became.

Why would I continue to give this man my power? Why would I devote even one more ounce of energy to him? Dr. Miller was right. Just recognizing that I was doing this was a huge help. My thoughts drifted to my mom—a woman who had been through so much pain and trauma of her own—first as a child, and then in her marriage to my dad, then in her marriage to HIM. I thought of her now, finally in a happy marriage with a man who treated her like she deserved and had been incredibly kind and generous to me over the years. It's true my mom had made a huge mistake in marrying my former stepdad. And it was wrong of her not to step up and protect her kids from him. But for the first time in my life, it occurred to me that maybe she had felt so beaten down and powerless herself that she hadn't been able to stand up for herself or her children. Was it fair of me to continue to punish her for a past that she couldn't change—no matter how much she wanted to? And if I continued to hold onto the anger and resentment, what was I accomplishing other than to make myself sick and cause her more pain when all she wanted was a relationship with me? I thought about my phone call asking her to come up and stay with Syd and Hannah for the week so I could visit Dr. Miller. She had jumped at the opportunity and thanked me for asking her to do it. She was doing everything she could do to build a relationship. The least I could do was wipe the slate clean.

On the final day of my visit with Dr. Miller, we were back in the patient room, once again seated in chairs across from each other.

By this point, I felt like I'd been through months of therapy. I no longer felt weak for delving into my painful past with Dr.

Miller and unleashing my emotions. I felt freer and more peaceful than I ever remembered feeling.

But I wasn't prepared for Dr. Miller's next pronouncement.

"There is a repeated negative behavior pattern among the women in your family," he said in a matter-of-fact tone. "You've got to be the one to break the pattern."

His words were like a slap on the face and threatened to undo that peaceful, fuzzy feeling I had inside.

"I can tell you one thing for sure," I snapped, feeling my face get hot. "I am not repeating my mom's patterns. For starters, my husband comes home every night and doesn't cheat. And I certainly didn't marry an abusive nightmare like she did with my stepdad. And I would NEVER let anyone hurt my daughters."

Dr. Miller didn't seem deterred. "Just think about it," he said as we parted ways.

I spent the entire evening mulling it over in my mind. How could he think I was repeating my mom's pattern? I was nothing like her. What did Dr. Miller mean?

I replayed his words over in my mind late into the night and the following morning. Then, while riding the train back to the airport, it hit me: I was like my mom in that I took on the entire financial burden and family responsibilities on my own. I never depended on John to help out. In fact, I shut him out and refused to count on him. Doing so would mean I was relinquishing my control.

John's words from that discussion a few months before screamed in my mind: *your biggest risk would be allowing yourself to depend on me.*

I thought back to when John and I met. He kept trying to pay for things and even though he earned more money than I did at the time, I always refused. It felt better when I paid. Doing so meant I maintained control of the situation.

Early on in our relationship, we took a two-week road trip to New Orleans. Because it was under the guise of my business, I insisted on covering all gas and lodging expenses along the way. I remember in New Orleans, I admired a sundress in a store window. John offered to buy it for me. I wanted that dress. But something inside me told me I couldn't let go of my control. I couldn't let him do that for me. So I refused and then felt bad the rest of the day.

Now, twelve years into our relationship and with two young daughters, the pattern had escalated to a point that it probably wouldn't have occurred to John anymore to just spontaneously want to purchase something for me.

I handled all the finances and paid all of the bills because I couldn't let go of that control. We never discussed money and at least from my point of view, it felt like John had checked out in that area. Though we were in a joint relationship, we operated separately. When John decided to accept the partnership offer at his firm, we never even had a conversation to discuss what kind of strain it would put on our finances or our relationship. And month after month when he was unable to draw a paycheck because his client receivables hadn't caught up enough to cover his share of the firm's overhead, he left it to me to figure out how to cover our bills. On top of that, he was rarely ever home. He was at his firm twelve hours a day, six days a week—leaving me to care for the girls on my own. When he arrived home in the evening, he was so burned out and tired he usually just plopped down in front of the TV for a couple of hours and then headed to bed. I knew he was depressed. And the stress of feeling like a single parent had been killing me. It was clear that this partnership wasn't working. But I hadn't known how to even broach it with him.

Dr. Miller's words played over and over in my mind. The realization that John and I were living separate lives—that I felt isolated, alone, and unable to communicate my concerns to him—was, at the moment, a lot scarier to me than my eye disease. I understood now what John meant when he said my biggest risk would be depending on him. I also understood that because I had been so controlling and independent from a financial standpoint, I had cut John out of the equation and the responsibility. We had to get on the same track. We had to start working as partners and start counting on each other. More than anything, I had to start counting and leaning on him. I still had the trust issue. And maybe I would lean on him and find out that he wasn't there for me. But I knew now that I would rather take the chance than continue living the way we were living.

Within a day of being home, I confronted John. I hated conflict and it was hard. It was also emotional. We both voiced hurt and pain from years of going it alone while living under the same roof. For several days, it felt like we were going head to head in a demolition derby.

But looking back, what stands out most is how quickly John was willing to do his part to step up once it was clear that I was serious about taking responsibility for my actions and changing my controlling ways.

Within a week of my return from my visit with Dr. Miller, John walked into his firm and gave his letter of resignation. He ventured into the world of self-employment on May 1, 2008— just before one of the worst financial crises in U.S. history, when companies everywhere pulled back on research and development, and work for patent attorneys was drying up.

7

Years ago I watched a *60 Minutes* segment on Ray Charles.

After capturing his life on tour and accompanying him to a typical sold-out concert where thousands of adoring fans shouted his name and sang along to his lyrics, Ed Bradley continued his profile of the world-famous blind musician at his home.

I was expecting a sprawling Beverly Hills mansion with a circular driveway, tennis courts, and a big fountain out front. Instead, Ray Charles lived in a modest apartment. The walls were bare and the rooms contained only a few basic pieces of furniture—a dining table, chairs, a sofa, bed, and dresser—all of which looked like they could have come from Ikea.

Neither Ed Bradley nor Ray Charles had to say it. The point was clear: if you couldn't see the expensive artwork, fancy handcrafted furniture, vaulted ceilings, or the lush, expansive landscape surrounding it, what did it matter?

When I was first diagnosed with RP, I didn't think much about this. I love beautiful things and when we moved into our Seattle house, all I could see were the endless cosmetic updates that needed to be made. But as I began my journey to fix my eyes by fixing my life, I started thinking more and more about that Ray Charles profile—about how much of what we think we need is tied to what we see around us. I began understanding just how much the pursuit of stuff blinds us from seeing what really matters and counts in life.

I don't think either John or I had any idea how much our life would change once he quit his job and started out on his own. But almost instantly, I felt like a huge pressure valve had been released.

That first morning on his own, John rummaged through our garage and unearthed an old metal desk that had once been used at Boeing. Together we pulled it into my small basement office and pushed it up against the wall directly across from my desk.

"Let's just hope this doesn't drive away the clients I had left," John said as he carried in boxes of client files and began organizing his side of the room. I knew he was concerned that it wouldn't look good for a patent attorney to be working out of his basement. But even as he said it, I could tell John was happy. Instead of wearing nice slacks and a button-down shirt, he was dressed in cut-off sweats and a T-shirt. And rather than having to fight through forty-five minutes of traffic to get to work, his commute now consisted of walking down the steps with a cup of coffee in hand.

The change in our relationship was just as dramatic. We went from rarely seeing each other to seeing each other constantly. We took morning coffee breaks and lunch breaks together and started talking and listening to each other again. We took turns walking our daughters to the bus stop and picking them up after school. And John began playing basketball at the local Boys and Girls

Club twice a week—a sport that had always been his passion but that he had essentially abandoned for ten years.

Our situation was even looking up financially. It might sound backward to quit your job and suddenly have money coming in, but because John had billed a bunch of client work at his firm that was no longer earmarked to cover his ever accruing firm overhead, the firm sent him the money as it was collected. That, in turn, helped us to cover costs while he got his solo practice off the ground. And though his client load had dropped to about a quarter of what it had been, it didn't hurt because we were used to pinching pennies and his overhead was now virtually non-existent.

Becoming financial partners had been a huge concern for me and I was worried that our past patterns would make this difficult to achieve. But it ended up being much less of an issue than I thought it would be. We agreed to start meeting once a week over coffee or a glass of wine to go through finances together. And even though money was still tight, just knowing that John was now mentally sharing the responsibility with me was a huge load off my shoulders. For the first time in our twelve years of marriage, we were actually operating as a team.

Probably the biggest lifestyle change for me was giving up driving. It wasn't a conscious decision. But with John now around to drive the girls to their various dancing, sports, and art activities, he began taking over that role and within a few months of his self-employment, it was a given that he would do all the driving.

I didn't realize until I stopped driving how much stress it actually caused me to get into the car, fight traffic, and constantly scan the roads, worrying about what I might be missing. Without the responsibility of driving Syd and Hannah around, I found myself walking everywhere throughout our neighborhood and loving it. It was only a mile walk to the gym, my two favorite coffee shops, and our local movie theater. Around the corner from our house was an independent movie rental store and ice cream shop, and across the street from there was a small neighborhood grocer. Everything I needed was within walking distance and it felt good not to have to depend on any transportation but my legs. It was a reminder of why we had moved to this house and neighborhood. I also discovered that walking required me to slow down and start paying attention to everything around me. For the first time since moving into the city, I noticed the different gardens and flowers in people's yards. I got to know where the dogs in the neighborhood lived and began to recognize their barks, some friendly, some not. I began to make friends with my neighbors— and not just the ones on my block.

My eyesight also seemed to be doing better. I was now diligently following Dr. Miller's extensive daily treatment program and I started sensing that my visual field was expanding a little. I began believing that I could really heal my eyesight.

"I'm thinking a year from now, my eyes are going to be so good I'll be able to drive again," I told John. "And you know what I want to do? I want to rent a red Mustang convertible and head out on a road trip for a week."

I'm not sure that John actually believed it. But he smiled at my conviction.

"It's a deal," he replied.

⌇

Though my life was now on the right track, I was still pounding away at my marketing communications business, even though every part of me yearned to put it aside and go after my writing dream.

Every six months or so, when the ache in my gut grew too strong to ignore, I would open up the manuscript of the coming-of-age memoir I had been working on for years and spend a few days writing. Then I would close the file and get back to my client work.

Talking about my childhood with Dr. Miller and letting go of the anger associated with it made me realize more than ever that I had a story I wanted to share. But though I had been more serious about enrolling in writing classes and critique groups, I was still unable to take the leap and make the commitment necessary to finish the book and start shopping it to agents.

I repeatedly told myself that it wasn't responsible to pursue my writing dream, not when we had two young daughters to support. I reminded myself that we couldn't swing it financially—that we were just getting by as it was and that it was even more risky to cut back on my client work now that John was also self-employed. Every once in a while when I got particularly discouraged, I would bring it up with John—something I had been doing over our entire marriage. And every time, the exasperation in his voice would grow louder.

"Look. If you want to write your book, write your book. We'll make it work. Just do it," he would say.

I would spend a day or two thinking about calling my clients and telling them that I was taking a break. Then I would tuck the dream away and throw myself into the safety and security of my marketing communications business.

I don't know why I couldn't trust that everything would work out if I let go of the control and gave myself permission to go after what I really wanted. Maybe it was because I was too scared of letting go of an income that came easily to me and seemed certain. Maybe, deep down, I worried that I wouldn't succeed as an author and that if I let myself actually go after it, this theory would prove itself. Deep down, I know I was still struggling to trust that if I completely depended on John financially for a bit, he would be there.

In the fall of 2009, John's business had grown enough that we felt it was time to go the next step and rent office space in our neighborhood. It was a little scary, but we figured if we were splitting the office rent between our two businesses, it would be easy to justify the money we were spending. After my continual teetering between my book writing dream and responsible marketing business, practicality once again won out and I decided to get serious about growing an agency. I had even hired a part-time employee to help me.

We moved into the office just before Thanksgiving and then took a weekend getaway with Syd and Hannah to celebrate the holiday.

It was evening and the four of us were walking down the street, searching for a family-friendly restaurant. Out of the blue, Syd and Hannah—then nearly eleven and eight—decided to do a parody of me as an old woman. Hannah, always the actor in the family, hunched over and pretended she was walking with a cane. Syd laughed and followed her lead.

I don't know if they conferred on this. But seconds later, in the most crotchety voices they could muster, they both yelled out in unison, "My book! My book! I have to finish my book!"

I felt like I'd been slapped across the face. Except that their words stung in a way that no physical blow could.

John, Syd, and Hannah all burst out laughing.

"You pegged her all right," John said, shaking his head.

I tried to laugh too. Just to prove I was a good sport. But inside I was mortified.

Was this what I was putting out into the universe? Was this what I was teaching my daughters? That you have a dream that's eating away at your soul but you don't go after it?

By the time dinner was over, I knew my current work life was over. The next morning, I asked John to accompany me for a morning coffee.

"I want to do it," I blurted. "I want to quit my client work and write my book. Are you really okay with it?"

John shook his head and laughed. "I knew that would get you. Yes. I've told you. We'll make it work. If you want to write your book, write your book."

This time, I wasn't going to lose my resolve. In January, I would be celebrating my forty-third birthday. I couldn't be in the same place when I turned forty-four.

John and I went over our finances and decided we could make it work if I reduced my workload by seventy percent. Within a month, I was down to one client and no employees.

I established a writing schedule to ensure that I made every second of my day count. Every morning I was up by 5:30 a.m. and managed to get in an hour of solid writing before stopping to make Syd and Hannah breakfast and get them out the door for school. Once they were off, I headed to the office I was still sharing with John and spent a couple of hours on client work. From there I headed to the gym to re-energize myself with a quick workout. Then it was back to the office for a fifteen-minute lunch break with John, then over to the coffee shop for two more hours of book writing before meeting Hannah at the bus stop.

By June, I had finished my manuscript. By early August, I had landed an agent—who encouraged me to start writing essays and building my author platform before she shopped my book to publishers. I felt like I owned the world.

⁂

SEPTEMBER – 2010

With everything else going so well in my life, I almost forgot about my eye disease. The treatment plan I was on seemed to be helping—at least my eyesight didn't seem to be getting any worse. I had been so busy focusing on my writing that I had slacked a bit on my treatment program. It was a lot of work to keep up on a daily basis and I just wanted to get on with my life.

Since receiving that devastating email from my friend a couple of years before, I'd stuck to my resolve to keep my vision issues a secret. When I bumped into an occasional chair or signpost, I passed it off as clumsiness. When I couldn't see a store clerk handing me back my credit card after a transaction, I pretended I was just absent-minded. Whenever parents at Hannah's elementary school questioned why I couldn't participate in fieldtrip car pools, I blamed it on a busy work schedule.

My strategy usually worked fine, though at a recent gym visit, I had encountered more than a few stares when I flew off the back of the treadmill I was running on because I didn't see my foot catch on the side of the machine. Back in the dressing room, I dropped my phone on the floor and couldn't find it. The woman next to me thought I was missing a few brain cells.

"It's right there," she said, as though I was supposed to know where "there" was.

"Where?" I asked, scanning the dark carpet an inch at a time.

"Right there on the ground in front of you. What's wrong with you? It's right there. You're practically stepping on it."

I left the gym embarrassed, but with my secret still intact. I figured the problem was my black phone case, which made it easy to blend in with the carpet. I made a mental note to shop for a neon green case as soon as I got the chance.

In mid-September, about a month after landing my agent, I was invited to a birthday celebration for a new friend. The party was held at a dimly lit neighborhood pub and was packed with people I hadn't met. As usual, I had a difficult time seeing faces— but I managed to at least make out an eye or nose and would always concentrate on that when talking with someone new.

Soon I was deep in conversation about the book industry with a wonderful woman I'd been introduced to by a mutual friend. She was a therapist who had written a self-help book and was anxious to learn about my book writing experience and how I had managed to secure an agent.

After talking for an hour, we parted ways and I inched my way through the maze of tables and chairs to the outside patio that was now illuminated with street lamps. I found John and began mingling with the crowd outside, enjoying the opportunity to connect with so many new people.

A half hour passed and John nudged me. "Ready to get going?" he asked.

"Sure, just fifteen more minutes," I replied. I was having such a good time and with a couple of glasses of wine in me, I was feeling especially social. There were so many people to meet. I scanned the outdoor crowd. My eyes rested on a woman I had noticed when I first arrived at the party. She looked interesting and I decided to introduce myself before I left.

I pushed my way through the crowd and positioned myself in front of her.

"Hi, I'm Ingrid," I said with a smile, extending my hand. "Just heading out but didn't get a chance to introduce myself and wanted to say hello."

The woman looked down at my extended hand and then back at me. Her face flickered from confusion to annoyance.

"Yeah. I know," she said finally. "We just talked for an hour."

I wanted to close my eyes, blink three times, and disappear. I felt my face turn hot with embarrassment. How could I be such an idiot? How was I going to talk my way out of this one?

The woman was staring at me, waiting for an explanation. Everything went quiet. I was certain that all of the people around us had overheard our exchange and that every eye was locked on me.

"Oh, I'm sorry," I mumbled. "I don't see well in the dark."

I quickly excused myself and pushed my way through the crowd until I found John.

"I'm ready to go. NOW."

I would have sprinted to the car if I could have seen where I was going. Instead, I had to wait for him to take my hand and guide me to it.

I tucked the humiliation away and redoubled my efforts to be more conscious and alert. I would just have to be more careful about talking to people in the dark.

Within a few weeks, I had brushed the incident aside. My agent had been schooling me on the new reality in publishing—the fact that it was nearly impossible to sell a manuscript from a new, unknown author. She stressed that publishers wanted to know that the author had a built-in audience ready to buy before gambling on the book.

I had taken the news in stride and was now focusing all of my efforts on building that audience. I had recently discovered Scribd.com, an open submission platform for writers and readers, and was starting to connect with its community of writers.

It was an evening in late October and I had just finished an online chat with one of my new writer friends. I said goodnight to Syd and Hannah and headed to the kitchen to make myself a cup of tea. I was so energized by the conversation that I was craving a good read and went searching through the house for my new issue of *The New Yorker.*

I cut through our long dark living room and made a U-turn around the wall divider that separated the living room from the hallway. My forehead hit the corner of the wall with such force it pushed me to the ground.

For a minute I was too stunned and in too much pain to move. My head felt like a hammer had been dropped on top of it. I pushed myself up to my knees and saw the pool of blood gathering on our rock tile entryway. I felt something wet drip into my right eye. My hand flew to my forehead and right eyebrow, and I felt the thick gash with blood going everywhere.

I cupped the wound with my hand, trying to contain the blood.

"John!" I yelled, still huddled on the floor holding my face. "I'm hurt. I need help."

Hannah came running down the hall first.

"Dad! There's blood everywhere," she called. "We need a towel quick."

Hannah and John went into action. Seconds later, John was on the floor next to me holding a towel to my forehead. Hannah scurried to the kitchen to make an ice pack.

"What in the hell happened?" John asked, removing the towel so he could examine the gash on my forehead.

"The wall ran into me," I muttered. "How bad is it?"

"Well, you'll live," John replied. "But you might not want to look in the mirror."

With Hannah working as his medical assistant, John used a butterfly bandage to squeeze the gash together on my forehead and eyebrow. I pushed myself to my feet and made my way to the bathroom mirror to check out the damage.

The woman gazing back at me looked like she had just been attacked. A long thick gash extended from the top right side of my forehead, cutting through my eyebrow and ending just above my right eye, which was already nearly swollen shut. I thought back to the car accident when I was twelve. Along with leaving the cluster of scars on my right forehead, the shattered glass had caught on the right corner of my lip and had left a clean rip clear up to the middle of my cheek. Though I had undergone plastic surgery to minimize the scar, it was still visible. Now I had another facial scar to add to my collection.

I stared at my reflection, lamenting what I saw looking back at me. I knew the gash could probably use a few stitches. But I didn't think it was worth the expense associated with heading to the emergency room. I kept staring at my battered face, thinking about the vertical scar that would now forever cut through my eyebrow. I don't know how long I stood there before another thought occurred to me: that a day might come when I wouldn't be able to see that scar or any other scar on my face.

The realization jolted me. It was like a switch had been turned on inside me.

For the first time since my diagnosis, I realized I wanted to talk about my struggles with my eyesight. I was tired of hiding my eye disease from the world. Tired of trying to pretend I could see what I couldn't. The constant cover up was exhausting and as I continued to take in my new wound and soon-to-be scar, I realized that maybe I had something worthwhile to share.

I spent the next week glued to my computer, working on an essay about my eye disease, about the initial fear and ongoing struggle, but also about the powerful life lessons I'd learned along the way—about learning to live in the present, pursue the work I was passionate about, and to see what was in front of me now.

When I finished the essay, I sent it to two writer friends I'd met through Scribd. I wanted their reaction and feedback before I shared it with a broader audience.

In the four months that we had been communicating via email—sometimes daily—I'd never once let on that I was legally blind and battling a degenerative eye disease.

Their reaction was shock. Then empathy. Then one of them, a former *New York Times* journalist who was in the process of shopping around her first novel, voiced the fear I had been carrying inside of me for the past six years.

"Are you going to use a pen name for this?" she asked in her email. "I mean, I just worry about you and I know how some people are out there. I just don't want this hurting your chances of finding a publisher. I know how important presentation is and I just want to make sure you are protected."

I loved her for her concern, for voicing what so few others would have had the guts to voice, for having my back. But after six years of hiding and worrying that people would think less of me if I disclosed my disability, I was done with the closet. I didn't know how people were going to respond. But I suddenly understood that maybe the only way to break through the stereotypes and uneasiness people had about blindness was to start talking about it and let the world know that behind the devastation of vision loss, there were normal people with the same hopes, dreams, and aspirations as everyone else. People who were doing everything they could to hold onto their eyesight, but who were also determined not to let it define them.

"Yeah, I've thought about it," I replied. "And I appreciate your concern. But I want to do this. If publishers don't want to take on my book because of my eye disease, I'll publish it myself. I'm tired of hiding this."

Three months later, my essay appeared as a front-page feature story on *Salon*. And the response was overwhelming. I don't know what I was expecting. I'd heard that *Salon* readers had a reputation for being mean and cutting in their comments. But in the flood of online comments and emails I received from readers, not one of them was disparaging or carried a trace of pity.

I was overwhelmed by the thank yous and well wishes from people who knew someone who struggled with blindness or who was dealing with a serious eye disorder or other devastating disease themselves. Or from people who simply were touched by my words and my decision to share my story and journey with the world.

As I read through the comments from strangers, I realized that it was my own prejudice against blindness that had kept me trapped in secrecy for the past six years. True, people have certain visceral responses to blindness. And there is no question that eyesight plays a crucial role in getting by in a very visually driven world. But what I discovered that day was that by openly discussing my eye disease, I was claiming my power over it. I also realized something else: that if I didn't have a problem with who I was, neither would anyone else. And if they did, so what?

8

"Mom, what would you wish for if you could wish for anything in the world?" Hannah asked me recently as we walked to the coffee shop for the regular reading and writing sessions that we both now enjoy.

"You know what I would wish for?" she interjected before I could answer. "I'd wish that you could see like everyone else."

Hannah, now ten, worries most about my eyesight. She's read every Helen Keller book she can get her hands on—maybe to assure herself that people can still survive if they're blind. She's internalized my vision problems in a way that no one else in my family has. Cleaning out her school folder recently, I came across a short story she had written about a blind girl who wished on a star that she could see. And the next morning she woke up with eyesight.

It's Hannah who reminds me to do my daily eye exercises, to stare into a color therapy lamp for a half hour at night when I'm tired, and to take all of my nutritional supplements. And it's

Hannah who most vocally verbalizes how much she wishes I could see like everyone else.

"It's just that then you could play catch with me and ride bikes," she explains wistfully. "You could also drive us when we need to go places."

Syd, now nearly fourteen, doesn't talk about it much. But recently she admitted to me that she's scared that maybe she's going to end up losing her eyesight too.

Because I have RP, medical statistics indicate that my daughters each have a fifty percent chance of suffering from RP as well. I'm convinced that years of chronic stress and poor nutrition have played a significant role in my degenerative eye disease and I hope that the healthy physical and emotional environment John and I are providing for our daughters will keep the disease at bay. But I know that something else is at play. Because despite my efforts to manage my stress, eat well, pump my body full of eye-focused nutritional supplements, and engage in every alternative therapy I can find, my eyesight still continues to slowly fade.

It's been eight and a half years since my first ever visit to an eye doctor revealed that I was legally blind. In that time, my visual field has shrunk from ten degrees in each eye to around two or three degrees (though I still pick up blurry images in a section of my outer periphery). What this means is that I now see only a small portion of what is directly in front of me—about the amount you would see looking through a hole the size of a silver dollar. And that's only when the light is good. When it's dark, even my severely limited central vision goes away.

Now when I look at my daughters and husband from across the table, I see only part of their faces. Sometimes when I walk into a room, I can't see them at all and have to listen to their voices to guide me to them. Simple daily tasks are becoming more and more difficult. When I sweep the floor, I often lose my pile and have to step away from it and scan the floor until I find it. John often insists on pouring my coffee for me because I've been known to miss the mug.

When we go to a movie now, my family has to arrive early so we can secure seats in the back row. That's the only way I can see the center of the screen. Even watching Syd play soccer or Hannah play ice hockey is difficult. The speed of both games makes it hard for me to track the ball or hockey puck—especially since I can only see a narrow part of the field or rink at any given time.

Though I'm an outgoing person by nature, it's a lot harder for me now to walk into a roomful of strangers and make the rounds because the faces become a blur and the crowds can be overwhelming. Even people I'm acquainted with sometimes mistake my inability to see them as rudeness. John's so used to fielding comments about this that he's started to play offense.

"Sorry. She's not ignoring you. She just doesn't see you," he'll jump in whenever he sees me fail to respond to a wave or to acknowledge someone who has been motioning to get my attention.

"But you don't act blind," people will often say when they first learn of my eyesight problems. "You seem completely normal."

Believe me, normalcy is what I'm aiming for. Though I no longer hide my eye disease, I don't want to have to always explain that I see life only an inch or two at a time.

Of all the hurdles that come with my failing eyesight, the one that currently affects my family the most is my inability to drive. While I enjoy walking, it's difficult not to be able to hop in a car to get where I need to go or to help John with the endless daily shuffle required to get Syd and Hannah to their respective sports practices.

Getting nearly anywhere without John requires navigating a bus system that is onerous and sometimes—based on the amount of alcohol consumed by fellow bus mates—feels unsafe.

Along with turning John into a nonstop chauffeur service, my inability to drive has forced me to depend on the generosity of others to get to work commitments and meetings not directly accessible by bus. It also means that friends who live on opposite ends of the city usually have to come my way for visits.

I want my eyesight.

I want it with every part of my being.

I want to see my daughters grow up—watch them get married and have children of their own. I want to be able to continue to take in the beautiful scenery around my neighborhood and to explore new cities and countries. I want to see John grow old—and I want to watch myself grow old with him.

On a fundamental level, I want to be able to see where I'm going.

Recently I had a conversation with a woman from my neighborhood who lost her eyesight to a stroke. She's an inspiring woman who teaches writing at a neighborhood senior center and seems to navigate the world fine with the seeing-eye dog that's always by her side.

"So what's on your bucket list?" she asked me.

"What do you mean?" I replied. I could already tell from the blood rushing to my face and my sudden clenched fists that I didn't like where this conversation was going.

"What are the things you want to do and see before you go blind?"

I know she was just trying to help. But her words stung. No matter how much my vision has faded, I just can't imagine a world without at least some eyesight.

"I guess I'm just focused on seeing," I managed.

She was quiet for a minute. "Well you've got to be prepared. That's just being practical."

Not long after, she invited me over for coffee so she could show me the accessible computer she uses. I appreciate her good intentions and I tried to talk myself into going. But I couldn't do it.

It's not that I'm sticking my head in the sand. But despite my limited vision, I have no interest in preparing to be blind. My energy is focused on seeing, and with so many medical advances now underway, I believe that a solution will materialize.

In Europe, eye doctors have started inserting microchips into the eyes of patients who have lost all of their eyesight to RP, and while resolution is limited, people who have been completely blind for years can now see shapes and outlines. Researchers recently reported that a chemical injected into the eyes of blind mice successfully restored their vision—at least for a few hours until the chemical wore off. At Johns Hopkins University, doctors working on animal models of RP have uncovered the cause of photoreceptor death in cone cells—those cells that are responsible for the central vision that I have left. This breakthrough is a huge step in figuring out a treatment that will preserve central vision in patients with RP. A large clinical trial is now underway to determine the benefits of Valproic Acid, an anti-seizure medication, in treating people who are battling RP. Extensive progress is also being made with gene therapies and stem cell research. And scientific studies are bearing out what Dr. Miller has been promoting for years: that addressing overall physical and emotional health are key components in slowing the progression of the disease.

With all the advancements being made, I'm confident that my daughters—if they do end up with this eye disease—will have a viable treatment available to them. And I'm hopeful that something soon will come along for me as well. Buoyed by the progress being made on the medical front and encouraging reports from a new friend who works for the Foundation Fighting Blindness, I've recently worked my way through insurance red tape to make an appointment (six months out) with a new retinal specialist who has been doing extensive research into stem cell therapies. In the meantime, I continue to integrate Dr. Miller's eye program into my daily life and am trying to be more diligent and consistent with it.

Dr. Miller's program has been a huge gift for me, in part because his emphasis on emotional and physical health has helped me to let go of past hurt and anger and improve my life, but also because the daily eye health regimen he recommends gives me something proactive I can do to help my eyesight now. I'm so grateful that I didn't give up when that retinal specialist told me there was no hope. And for anyone else out there who has been told the same, please consider these wise words that Dr. Miller once shared with me, "Always remember that when doctors tell you that 'nothing can be done for you', what they are really saying is that 'there is nothing THEY can do for you.'"

Along with doing all I can to preserve my remaining eyesight, what I've learned in managing my eye disease is that I'm fine as long as I concentrate on the moments in front of me and think about everything I have to be grateful for in life. It's when I let myself worry about the future that fear and panic set in.

I often think of Eckhart Tolle's powerful words in his book, *The Power of Now*. The gist is this: you can't control the future or change the past. So if you spend your time and thoughts there, you are likely to live in a state of unhappiness and fear. But if you live fully in the present, you can always manage to get through

THE NOW. This has proven true in my own life. Back when I was first diagnosed, dwelling on the idea that I would eventually have only two or three degrees of vision in each eye would have landed me in a loony bin. But the fact is that despite the challenges, I do fine. And my life is so much better now than it was eight and a half years ago that I wouldn't trade what I have now to regain that extra eyesight and go back to who I was then.

My fading eyesight has taught me to look at my daughters and really see them and hear them. We've developed an amazing friendship and bond, and I've been able to watch them both grow into beautiful young women—not just on the outside, but on the inside.

Because of my eye disease and the lessons my daughters and husband have taught me along the way, I've learned to go after my dreams now and not wait for a future when the money and stars line up—or when someone else gives me permission. And I've discovered that when you go after what you are truly passionate about, the Universe has a way of opening up paths for you.

After a year of platform building to make it easier for my agent to sell my manuscript to publishers, I decided to embrace the fast-emerging indie publishing world driven by eBooks and print-on-demand. I hired an editor and designer and published my memoir on my own in the fall of 2011.

In January of 2012, after devoting two years to my writing dream, I took the final step by parting ways with my last remaining client and wrapping up my marketing communications business for good. That same month, Marjie Bowker, a gifted high school English teacher who thrives on making education relevant and powerful for her students, invited me to form an author partnership with her. Together, we used my coming-of-age memoir as a guide to help her at-risk teen students claim their power by finding their voice and sharing their stories. I worked with Marjie to help the students publish their stories in a powerful teen anthology that is now making an impact on teens across the country. The experience was so empowering that Marjie and I are continuing our partnership. We also hope to expand our mentoring/publishing program to other schools and teen organizations. I'm now so excited about the work I'm doing that I can't wait to get up in the morning and get started. John feels the same way about his law practice, and it's a life lesson that is not lost on either Syd or Hannah.

"It's like you and Dad retired early," Syd said to me recently. "I mean, it really is true because now you just do what you love to do anyway so it's really not work. That's what I want for my life."

Probably the most valuable—and difficult—life lesson for me has been learning to trust and let go. In doing so, I've strengthened my relationships with John and everyone else around me. I've discovered that accepting help doesn't make me weak—that it actually takes a lot of strength to be vulnerable. I've also discovered that letting down my walls makes it easier for others to let down their walls and to share their own challenges and struggles.

While you might not know it by looking at them, I've learned that nearly everyone has something serious they are dealing with in their lives. For some of us, it's a devastating disease. For others, it's a family member with a terminal illness. For still others, it's the death a loved one. Then there's Nathanda, Thandi and the others I met in South Africa.

It's impossible to understand why some people are forced to endure so much. But what I've learned is that none of us are immune to disease and death, and that life can change in an instant. We can't predict the future—not even five minutes into the future. What we have for sure is Now. And because I finally understand how precious Now is, I'm determined to make the most of it.

Our house still has the same popcorn ceilings and pink and blue toilets that it had when we moved into it. But instead of seeing the cosmetic imperfections, looking at them reminds me of how far I've come in my life.

It's been incredible watching Syd and Hannah embrace the changes in our family. Our relaxed lifestyle means that we get to spend lazy summer days together—enjoying walks to the library, afternoons at the park, or spur-of-the-moment lunch dates with John.

While we rarely shop and have cut back on eating out, we've incorporated special family traditions such as Free Friday—which involves a trip to the grocery store where everyone is allowed to choose their dinner of choice; or family movie night where we all crawl into the master bedroom's king-size bed with a movie from the corner video store and two salad bowls packed with popcorn.

My family wants my eyesight as much as I do. They all occasionally express their frustration over the challenges it poses, and Hannah—in particular—is constantly on the lookout for new eye treatments that will benefit me. But maybe because of this journey we've all been on, they are the first ones to steer me back into the present whenever I slip and find myself getting discouraged over having to see life through a straw.

"Don't think about what you've lost—focus on what you can still see," John will say when he catches me feeling down.

"Yeah, Mom, remember Africa," Syd or Hannah will chime in. "It's not like you are dying or starving to death. You've got a great life and you get to do the work you love. And you have us."

Talk about a depression killer. It's impossible to stay down when I'm reminded of just how much I have.

I often think back to what my dad said all those years ago: *when something is taken away from you, something else is given in its place.*

It took me a while to learn, but I know now he was right. With no peripheral vision to distract me, I've been forced to focus on what's right in front of me—my family, my friends, my dreams, this moment.

I wouldn't have guessed that the replacement gift my dad assured me of would come as a direct result of my fading eyesight. But I do know that it's the most valuable gift I could have been given. And as long as I treasure it and keep it with me, I know it's something no amount of vision loss can take from me.

ACKNOWLEDGEMENTS

Every day I thank the Universe for my husband, John, and our two daughters, Sydney and Hannah. They are such amazing gifts and have taught me what matters. This book wouldn't exist without them.

I also owe a huge thank you to Risa Laib, a gifted editor who donated her talent and time to help me better communicate the story I wanted to tell, and to Suzanne Nelson and Dr. Damon Miller, who both took time out of their busy schedules to serve as fact checkers.

Thanks also to Laura Pepper Wu and Malachi Jones for reading through early drafts and offering valuable feedback, to Juli Saeger Russell for the amazing cover design and typesetting, and to Jennifer D. Munro, for her careful eye.

Finally, thank you to Stephanie Durden Edwards, Suzanne Rosenwasser and Laura Novak, for navigating this writing journey with me, Mari-Ann Kind Jackson, for showing me by example how to live in the moment, and Marjie Bowker, who changed the course of my work life when she invited me into her classroom to work with her students.

My Amazing Family

ABOUT THE AUTHOR

Ingrid Ricks started her career as a journalist, spent fifteen years as a marketing/PR consultant, and is now embracing her writing/mentoring dream full-time. She is the author of the coming-of-age memoir, *Hippie Boy: A Girl's Story*, and a short memoir story collection, *A Little Book of Mormon (and Not So Mormon) Stories*.

Through her partnership with high school English teacher Marjie Bowker, Ingrid recently helped at-risk teens publish their personal stories in a powerful collection titled *We Are Absolutely Not Okay: Fourteen Stories by Teenagers Who Are Picking Up the Pieces*. That project has led to the launch of www.WeAreAbsolutelyNotOkay.org, a web site devoted to helping teens connect with other teens through personal storytelling.

Ingrid lives in Seattle with her husband and two daughters. When not writing, working with students, or leading seminars focused on embracing the moment, she can be found accompanying her family to soccer games, ice hockey games, or the beach. She also enjoys hanging out at her neighborhood jazz club or alternating between her two favorite coffee shops. For more information, visit www.ingridricks.com.

CPSIA information can be obtained at www.ICGtesting.com
Printed in the USA
BVOW031824081112

304981BV00002BA/2/P